We Played Our Cards

Overlake Publishing
P.O. Box 4607
Burlington, VT 05406-4607

ISBN 0-9744463-0-0

Printed in the United States of America

We Played Our Cards

by Joseph Edward Corbett

The Navy Diver is not a fighting man.

He is a salvage expert.

If it's lost underwater he finds it.

If it's sunk, he brings it up.

If it's in the way, he moves it.

If he's lucky, he dies young
Two hundred feet beneath the waves.

Cause that is the closest he will
Ever get to being a hero.

Hell, I don't know why anybody
Would want to be a Navy Diver.

— *Billy Sunday, Master Chief Navy Diver*
  (portrayed by Robert DeNiro in the film Men of Honor*)*

*Dedicated to my family
and my friends.*

—JEC

Contents

Prologue

During the early years of the war in Europe and the rise of the Nazi Party (to use Tom Brokaw's phrase) the "Greatest Generation of Americans" was going to high school and entering college. We were on the sidelines and observing the relentless aggressiveness of a dictatorial paper hanger, Adolf Hitler, whose genius for manipulation grabbed the heartstrings of a nation and squeezed from them a fanatical loyalty. We were going through the usual high school experiences of some studying, participating in high school athletics and drama, and generally getting ready for college or preparing for the workforce.

In 1940 we suddenly experienced the first peacetime draft, that by war's end in 1945 had evolved into the participation of 16 million Americans. As the rise of Hitler and persecution of the Jews continued, our generation became aware of the ominous cancer spreading throughout the world. I will never forget September 1, 1939, when the wholesale killing began. Hitler's deputies then unleashed, on Poland, one and a half million German soldiers backed by the most powerful war machinery ever known to man. I was a senior in high school and for the first time in my life I was aware of humans killing their counterparts in open war. Young men of my age were killing other young men. This was the grim reality of war. My life took on a new aspect and preparing for a far-off war in Europe now appeared to be our future.

The young men and women of this generation were about to participate in the most intensive game of, and for, their lives. None of us really knew what our future might hold. What we were to do in college or life after high school would surely lead us to some sort of participation in World War II. So we sat down to the dealing of the cards and prepared to play them as they were dealt.

Many of my friends in high school went on to college and others, for many reasons, entered other careers. Some of my high-school friends joined the CCC (the Civilian Conservation Corps) a federal project engaged in conservation projects throughout the country. These were the only jobs many young men could get during those years following the depression. I was fortunate to enroll in college and prepared for a degree in engineering.

The purpose of putting down on paper my experiences and those of other close friends is to relate how our lives evolved and were connected through the years of World War II. Every anecdote and story of their lives is the actual history of what the war did to many of the people who touched my life. It is of what happened to us, and how we played the cards that were dealt. Whether fate chose to send us to the battlegrounds of Europe or the Pacific islands, or enlisted us for support at home, we had to serve our country in whatever role was demanded of us.

Many of my friends did not come back, losing their lives in far corners of the world. Some came home with mental or physical problems indelibly affecting their lives. Those war years did something to all of us, but our participation is what had to be done. We all managed to serve our country in some form or other, in whatever role we were needed.

In any case, "We played our cards."

Mom, Jim, Mike, Loretta, Tom, me and Dad

The Early Years

first saw the light of day on February 15th, 1921, in the town of North Tonawanda, New York. This was a relatively small town on the Niagara River between Buffalo and Niagara Falls. The country was reeling from the Great War and striving to get back to normal.

There were 8 million horseless carriages – the Model T had been around since 1908. Most of them were Ford Tin Lizzies, that cost $300. Radios were becoming the real thing. In that year the first Miss America was crowned from a field of eight contestants. Prohibition was about two years old and Al Capone was becoming a big shot in Chicago. Lynching continued thru the '20s and the Klan was a mainstream organization. Rudolph Valentino was starring in *The Sheik*.

I was the youngest of four boys – Mike, Tom, Jim, and Joe. A few years later Loretta arrived, the first girl. Also living with us at that time was Grandpa Burns, my mother's father – one of my most unforgettable characters. My dad was 30 years old. He had been a pattern maker since he was about 14 years old, when he left school to support his mother and sister after his dad had died. Both of his parents were born in Ireland and immigrated in the late 1800s. He was operating a pattern shop in the top floor of a large building occupied by the Herschell Spillman Corporation, that made amusement rides and the first of the famous carousels. One of the big thrills then was to ride on the first models of the Lindy Loop, the Hay Day, the Caterpillar among others. The roller coaster was an innovation with a future.

We all went to Ascension School and were taught by the Sisters of St. Joseph. My first year of kindergarten was in a public school as Ascension ran from first grade through the first year of high school.

Lindbergh flew from New York to Paris, leaving on May 20th in 1927. Babe Ruth started hitting homers about this time. These two guys were my first real heroes. Al Smith, "the Happy Warrior in the

Mike, myself, Loretta, Jim and Tom at Mike & Margaret's 50th Wedding Anniversary in 1989

Our Boy Scout Drum corps

Brown Derby," a Democrat and the first Roman Catholic to run for President, was defeated by Herbert Hoover in 1928. I remember Dad was a dyed-in-the-wool Democrat in those days. The Depression hit in 1929, bringing with it years of tough times for everybody. In 1932, Franklin D. Roosevelt defeated Herbert Hoover overmatched by circumstance.

These were trying years as the pattern business was hit along with all other industry in the country. I was in grade school and my brother Jim and I both had paper routes. We all pitched in at home. I remember many meals of fried baloney, lots of hamburgers, and plenty of homemade pies. We had a great garden in the backyard. Grandpa Burns did most of the planting and hoeing, with some help from us kids.

In Germany, the Nazi party had about 210,000 members and the book *Mein Kampf*, was selling briskly. I was in the seventh grade about that time and my brothers Jim, Tom, and I were in the Boy Scouts. We did a lot of camping along with the usual Scout activities including our drum corps. Several summers, about five of us would go up to the Adirondack Mountains around Raquette Lake, rent a couple of canoes, and camp around the lake for two weeks.

Here is an excerpt from a book written by one of our campers, Ed Duquette in 1992.

After graduation a vacation was in order. And we picked Raquette Lake in the Adirondack mountains for our camping trip. Tom Corbett, his brothers Jim and Joe, and my brother Allan were going. All of us were members of Boy Scout troop No. 79. We were expert campers by this time, especially Tom the oldest of all of us and the one with the car. Raquette is buried in the Adirondacks surrounded by pines and sandy beaches. We found a camp site on the lake shore, put up our tents and went to the country store to rent two canoes for two weeks. Tom drove the car back while the rest of us paddled to our camp site and beached the canoes, just like real Indians. Camping was really roughing it— no lights, refrigerator or even a Coleman stove. A deep hole in the ground refrigerated our slabs of bacon. Every morning we had bacon sandwiches and coffee.

Have you ever paddled a canoe like an Indian on a mirror smooth lake – careful how you dip your paddle not to cause ripples. We are trailing a flock of geese swimming in single file. The last goose, the lookout, leaves the line and swims up to the leader and suddenly the squadron is in the air flying abreast – better than the Blue Angels. This was nature study at its best.

We went back every summer repeating the same experiences telling all the old jokes, with some new ones, paddling around the same lake until the year 1939. Returning home, from a fun two weeks with friends, the radio broadcast the invasion of Poland. Our fun was over.

I saw Tom Corbett at our 50th reunion in 1987. We had fun reminiscing about our camping trips to Raquette Lake. Tom died recently and I know he is in heaven watching the geese fly in formation and telling St. Peter how to make bacon sandwiches.

My brother Tom was a special kind of guy as he was partially handicapped from about the age of eight. He was riding on a bobsled and fell off, injuring his hip. The bruise developed into an infected bone and then tuberculosis. Modern medicine could have cured this infection with penicillin or an antibiotic but in those days an operation was required. He had several operations but the results of the injury was that one leg was about three or four inches shorter than the other. He used crutches for a while, but a later development of a special shoe allowed him to walk much better. It was amazing how well he could get around. He pitched for our baseball team and when he was the batter someone would stand next to him – when he got a hit they would run for him. After he graduated from high school he entered the pattern shop as an apprentice to my father. He learned this trade, was an excellent pattern maker, and eventually took over the business when my father passed away.

As soon as I was able to do something besides the paper route, I got jobs in drug stores, grocery stores, and on Saturdays Dad had me clean up all the shavings and wood pieces at the pattern shop.

Thomas Andrew Burns

Grandpa Burns, my mother's dad, lived with us and was the eighth member of our family. He had been born in Thorold, Ontario, the son of Irish immigrants. One of his early jobs was driving horses on the Welland Canal connecting Lake Erie with Lake Ontario. Those horse teams would tow the barges through the canal from tow roads adjacent to the canal. He also worked in stone quarries as a stone-cutter and laborer.

He had three daughters from his first marriage, and when his wife died he remarried and moved to North Tonawanda, New York. As long as I could recall, Grandpa was quite deaf. There were no hearing aids then and we could only communicate by shouting to him. He was wonderful to us kids and I could never remember him admonishing or being angry with any of us. He was a very religious Catholic and I remember him quietly sitting in his chair, smoking a pipe and saying his rosary beads. Taking him to confession at our local church was an event. Being so deaf, he would essentially shout to the priest and his confessions were audible to people in the near-by pews – gratefully, nothing much very exciting.

He was a feisty little guy and often told the story about coming home from work at the quarry one day when he was apprehended by a would-be robber who pulled a gun on Grandpa and demanded,

Grandpa Burns with Aunt Kate and Mother

"Your money or your life!" With that Grandpa swung his lunch pail, hit the guy in the face, and said "Take my life, you bastard – I'm saving my money for my old age!" Apparently the guy fled because Grandpa was still around.

Another time during the early war years I was in the kitchen with my mother and grandpa was reading the newspaper. It was in the summer of 1941, soon after the United States had entered the war. He looked up from the paper and said, "I guess Hilter (Hitler) is giving Johnny Bull (England) a damn good beating". He said this with a chuckle because he was pretty much living in the past. His memories of the old potato famine years, the Easter Rebellion and Finian Raids had left an indelible mark in his mind about the British treatment of the Irish. Some of these memories of the old days had left their impression on old timers like Grandpa. If he had been eligible during WWII, I'm sure he would be a fighting U.S. Marine and beat the hell out of "Hilter". It was soon after that, when Jim and I were to join Johnny Bull in his fight against "Hilter".

One day I took Grandpa to the barber for a shave and a haircut. There were about five or six people in the barbershop including a couple of ladies with their little kids. As the barber was cutting his hair he began a conversation with Grandpa. He became aware of the barber's efforts to communicate with him and said in a loud voice, "No use talking to me, I'm so damned deaf I can't hear myself fart, the only way I can tell is by the jar." I kind of cringed in the corner, several of the men chuckled, and the ladies with their kids were mortified.

Grandpa Burns lived to the ripe old age of 92 and in later years he obviously had what we now call Alzheimer's. In those days the doctors said the mental deficiency was a product of hardening of the arteries. His memory will always be with us as he was a major part of all our lives.

When I started high school, my brother Mike, who was about six years older than I, was working at the Columbus McKinnon Chain Company. Obviously in those years of the Depression, going to college was out of the question. During that time he had aspired to an engineering future and was taking a correspondence course in drafting and mechanical drawing. In following years he was employed at the Wurlitzer Corporation, a manufacturer of organs and jukeboxes. With that company he was an engineer instrumental in the design and building of the famous Wurlitzer jukebox. He was married in 1939 to Margaret Graham and raised a wonderful family of four girls and two boys.

While I was in high school two of my closest friends were David Graham and Chet Behrns. Dave and I published a small newspaper called *The Gassette*. Dave was a good cartoonist and I did most of the writing. The Depression and uncertain economic conditions contributed greatly to its demise, ceasing publication after two issues.

I was on the basketball squad, the 11th of about a dozen guys. I also was manager of the football team. Charlie Pacini and Don Kasprszak, buddies of mine, played both sports. We also played baseball together. Charlie was in our Scout troop and went on one of our Raquette Lake trips. Don eventually went to Columbia University and was a star quarterback before entering the Marines. Charlie went to Niagara University on a football scholarship and became a Marine in 1942.

I graduated from high school in 1938 but took a postgraduate year in 1939 in order to take Chemistry and Physics. The following fall of 1939 I headed for the Green Mountains and joined my brother Jim at the University of Vermont.

Hometown Friends In World War II

North Tonawanda, New York

Chester Behrns – U.S. ARMY – *North Tonawanda, New York*

Chet and I were close friends during our high-school years. My recollections are that he was a big Benny Goodman fan and we listened to a lot of swing in those years. After we left high school I went to the University of Vermont and Chet worked for a big sporting goods store in Buffalo. He sold me my first golf clubs for a helluva discount.

Early in May of 1942 Chet enlisted in the army Infantry and became a unit commander in the 25th infantry Division in the South Pacific. His division participated in the liberation of the Philippines and the battles of Luzon. He was discharged in March 1946 having earned a Silver Star, a Bronze Star, and the Combat Infantry badge for the South Pacific. In November of 1950 he returned to active duty in Korea and participated in the spring counteroffensive in that war. He was discharged in March of 1952 having been a unit commander of the Seventh Infantry Division in Korea. He was awarded the Bronze Star and the Combat Infantry badge with star for his service during the Korean conflict. Chet has retired and is living in Florida. We still keep in touch.

Chet's wife Betty was a Pharmicist's Mate 3rd Class in the U.S. Navy Waves from December 1943 until November 1945, serving as a nurse at Hunter College and Great Lakes Naval Station. Chet and Betty served their country with major contributions during their marriage.

Charles Pacini – U.S. MARINE CORPS – *North Tonawanda, New York*

Charlie and I grew up together, were in the Boy Scouts, and played basketball and baseball in high school. When I went to the University of Vermont, Charlie came up the following year on a football scholarship but later transferred to Niagara University. In 1942 he enlisted in the Marines, went to the South Pacific and with Edson's First Marine Raiders struck at Tulagi in the Guadalcanal landing. During these operations Charlie was seriously cut by a saber and lost two fingers in a hand-to-hand fight with a Japanese soldier. He was also wounded in the leg and neck. He was discharged in 1945, having been decorated with the Gold Star, Purple Heart, and the Presidential Citation Bar.

In later years Charlie became an outstanding high school football coach in New Jersey. One of his more famous students was Dick Lynch, the great defensive back with the New York Giants professional football team. Charlie passed away several years ago.

Donald T. Kasprzak – U.S. MARINE CORPS – *North Tonawanda, NY*

One of my closest friends in high school was Donald Kasprzak. Don was an outstanding quarterback on our football team and also excelled in basketball and baseball. He went to Columbia on a football scholarship and was one of their great quarterbacks. He enlisted in the Marine V12 program in March 1942. He was with the Fourth Marine Division in Hawaii as a second lieutenant in the infantry. We met in Pearl Harbor while our ship the *Preserver* was in drydock and had a great get-together. He was later with the first Marine Division Pioneer Batallion as an intelligence officer when they went to Northern China. Don was discharged in 1946 and went back to medical school at Columbia University and graduated in 1951. Don is a thoracic surgeon in Plattsburg, New York, and we still keep in touch with each other.

Sherwood Sutton – U.S. ARMY – *North Tonawanda, New York*

Red Sutton was in high school with me and grew up in our neighborhood. He always wanted to go to West Point as he was very interested in a military career. He subsequently went to college and enlisted in the army in 1942. During World War II, his unit participated in the Okinawa campaign on the island of Ie Shima. I do not know the details but have been told by several of my friends that when Ernie Pyle was killed April 18th, 1945 by a sniper's bullet, Red Sutton participated in that action and lost an arm. Several years after World War II, I visited with Red and his wife Lida and he had a hook prosthesis for the arm he lost at Ie Shima. He was one of the many brave young men I knew who returned from the war with a tragic disability.

David Graham – *North Tonawanda, New York*

Not everyone of us was called to serve in the armed forces. There were many who participated in the war effort, working in essential industries. After graduating from high school Dave went to work for the Bell Aircraft Company in Niagara Falls, New York. He rapidly moved up in this organization and worked closely with Larry Bell, the president. During the war that company produced several of our great combat fighter planes, including the Airacobras, that were instrumental in defeating the German and Japanese air power.

Robert Leo Measer – U.S. ARMY AIR FORCE – *Buffalo, New York*

You seldom have any choice in selecting your in-laws, but if I could have chosen my little sister's husband, Bob Measer would have been the guy. My sister Loretta and Bob were married in 1951. He had been a fireman in the Buffalo Fire Department since his discharge from the army air force in September 1945.

Bob Measer

In February 1943, he volunteered for the United States Air Force. His early flight training was in Fairchild PT-23s, at the air force base in Cape Girardeau, Missouri, from December 13, 1943, to February 5, 1944. He then had twin-engine training in Stuttgart Army Airfield, Arkansas. He received his commission as a second lieutenant in June 1944. From July 4th at Laredo Texas until December 3rd he was trained to fly B-24 Liberator bombers, America's second generation heavy bomber. These bombers had greater range than the B-17s and were superior in speed and payload. Nineteen thousand of them were produced during World War II.

In January 1945, he was sent to Nadzab, New Guinea and piloted his B-24 on six combat missions to Weiwak, Rabaul, and Hollandia. From New Guinea his bomber squadron was transferred to Mindoro Air Force Base in the Philippines.

From February 21st to August 15, 1945, he flew 43 missions to Formosa, Saigon, Matsuyama, Toshein, Kiirun, Shinchiku, Taihoku, Taichu, and Balikpapan.

Following are some of the entries in his flight log after some of those missions:

March 2nd from Mindoro to Formosa to Luzon to Mindoro. First close call was on March 2nd when we came back from Formosa low on gas. Not being able to make it home we landed on Luzon with about 25 gal. in both tanks. First flak hole, three ships holed.

April 8th from Mindoro to Formosa. Second close call was again coming from Formosa. Due to terrible weather the formation got separated. We took up a heading that we thought would get us to Luzon. After exceeding our ETA by one and one-half hours our navigator found by taking sun shots we were east of Luzon. We took up a heading of South West and after flying for an hour could not see land in sight. The gas was low and everybody was ready to jump if we couldn't make it. Then we sighted Luzon and followed the coast down. The weather was terrible and we didn't know whether we had enough gas to climb over the mountains. However we took up a course to Linguayan Gulf and the gas held out till we landed there. We had about 25 gal. of gas left.

April 14th from Mindoro to Carabro. Milk run. Wonderful bombing Shinsosai Airdrome. Saw one ship explode. Fighter interception.

April 20th from Mindoro to Saigon, Indochina. Missed Japanese Heavy Cruiser. Flak heavy. Fighter made feeble pass. Ship holed.

May 15th Mindoro to Shinchiku. Target clear. Lots of flak. Lost No. 2 engine on return. Landed at Clark #1.

May 31st to Mindoro to Taihoku to Mindoro. Flak really rough. One hole in plane.

June 15th Mindoro to Taichu to Mindoro. One flak hole below my feet

July 12th Mindoro to Shien to Mindoro. Rough target. Major Dyson shot down.

On July 22nd his group flew to Okinawa and did patrol combat time between Japan and Okinawa. They also ferried prisoners of war from Okinawa via Guam and Kwajalein to Oahu. Then on October 16, 1945, he flew his B-24 from Oahu to Port of Aerial Debarkation, Mather Field, California and was soon discharged.

Bob was awarded the Army Air Force Air Medal for meritorious achievement during flight. His certificate reads:

For Meritorious Service – The Commanding General Army Air Forces extends the gratitude of the United States Army Air Forces to flight officer Robert Measer whose wholehearted and sincere services contributed to the successful prosecution of World War II against those who sought to subjugate the civilized world.

It was signed by "Hap" Arnold, Commanding General of the Army Air Forces.

Bob and my sister Loretta were married in 1951. They had a son Robert and two daughters, Mary and Anne. They have four grandsons and six granddaughters. Bob passed away in 1985 and Loretta died in 2001 after over 25 years bravely battling multiple sclerosis. We miss two wonderful and loving people.

The Nilands – *Tonawanda, New York*

I grew up in the town of North Tonawanda, New York, which is just across the Erie Barge Canal from Tonawanda. Both of the cities had populations intensely involved in athletics. Consequently there was a rivalry between the high schools of both cities and other groups participating in competitive sports.

The most significant rivalry was between the football teams of both high schools. Historically that "neck of the woods" had produced excellent athletic teams for many years. The annual Thanksgiving Day game between the football teams was the sports event of the year. Every year our football teams battled area rivals for the Western New York championship. Quite often the crown rested on the winner of the annual Turkey Day classic between the Tonawandas.

Thanksgiving dinner was always preceded by the big game. We had a family of eight and when we sat down to carve the turkey we were either elated or dejected, depending on the outcome of the football game. My brother Mike and I, being of slight stature, did not participate in football but played baseball and basketball. Jim at over six feet tall played football, while Mike and I were managers.

My dad of course was our biggest fan in all of our athletic endeavors. Brother Tom had a crippled leg and could not play. Mother and our younger sister Loretta bravely endured the adventures of the "jocks" in the family. although the term "jocks" was never used in those days.

Through the years and with our involvement in sports the Corbetts quite often found themselves competing with members of the Niland clan from across the canal. We had kind of a "Hatfields and McCoys" friendly rivalry. In the church baseball league, our parish team from Ascension quite often played the Tonawanda parish team, St. Francis. Or in later years the NT Alumni or Blue Danube baseball team would play the Eldredge Club from Tonawanda. This athletic rivalry also involved the high school basketball teams. Invariably in many of these intense rivalries on the opposing teams would be a Corbett and a Niland. The Nilands by sheer numbers exceeded the Corbetts as they had the advantage of drawing from two families. One family had Bill, Tom, and Jim. The other had Ed, Bob, Fritz, and Pete.

One year I vividly remember when my brother Mike was playing second base and Bill Niland slid into second, a la Ty Cobb. Mike came up with a broken nose. Traditionally when our high-school basketball team played Tonawanda, my brother Jim was assigned to guard Joe Niland, their high scorer. Most often Jim held him to single figures. When our baseball team batted against Joe, who was a left-handed pitcher and threw a wicked curve, I was never able to hit off him. Another year Tom Niland and I played on the same American Legion baseball team when we played against Lockport in the county finals. Tom played shortstop and I played second. Some time ago when LeMoyne College played St. Michael's basketball team in Burlington, Vermont, Tom was coaching LeMoyne. I visited him on the bench and we renewed our old acquaintance.

We did however have some cordial friendships with some of the members of the other Niland family. Fritz and Bob were fraternity brothers in the Sigma Psi fraternity as we had started another chapter in Tonawanda. We quite often had joint meetings and social events between the two chapters. Tom, Jim, and I were members of the North Tonawanda Sigma Psi.

In World War II the Niland families distinguished themselves with the same fervor and competitiveness as they had displayed in their athletic efforts.

The movie *Saving Private Ryan* was about the World War II experiences of the Niland brothers. Although the movie was fictional there was a real paratrooper in the 101st Airborne Division whose family suffered the loss of three out of four sons in combat, in a short period of time. This was the Niland family and the basis of the movie.

The movie was developed from an event that took place in Fr. Francis Sampson's book, *Look Out Below!* (pages 78-79). This is what

Fr. Sampson wrote:

When the regiment was bivouacked near Utah Beach waiting for the boats to take us back to England, a young soldier by the name of Fritz Niland came to see me. He was very troubled in mind. The company commander of his brother, who was with the 508th Regiment, told Fritz that his brother had been killed and was buried in the Sainte-Mere-Eglise cemetery. We jumped in my jeep and drove the twenty miles back to that town. In checking the cemetery roster I couldn't find the boys name.

"There's no William Niland listed here Fritz,' I said encouragingly, 'though there is a Roland Niland listed."

"Father… that's my brother too. He was a lieutenant in the 90th Division." The unhappy boy tried to choke back the tears. After saying a few prayers at the grave, we went to another cemetery just a few blocks away where we found the grave we were looking for originally. A third brother had just been killed in the Pacific.

As we were driving back to the bivouac area, Fritz kept saying over and over again, more to himself than to me, "What will poor Butch do now? What will poor Butch do now?"

"Who is Butch, son?" I asked.

"Butch? Oh, she's my mother." I looked at him and wondered if he were suffering from combat exhaustion and the terrible shock of this afternoon's discovery. He must have read my thoughts, for he explained, "We four boys always called Mom 'Butch' these last few years. That's because, when we wanted to listen to swing orchestras and jive bands on the radio, Mom would always turn on 'Gangbusters' or some other program about gangsters… she liked those. Now I'm the only son left." Mrs. Niland had received three tragic wires within a week, however, we managed to get Fritz sent back to the States, so Butch still had one son to comfort her.

Sgt. Frederick "Fritz" Niland who had been awarded a Bronze Star Medal, was a member of the 101st Airborne's 501st Parachute Infantry Regiment and was one of those that made the drop into Normandy on June 5th and 6th, 1944.

Fritz's three brothers served in other units. Technical Sergeant

Robert Niland with the 2nd Airborne Division (505th Parachute Infantry Regiment), Lieutenant Preston Niland with the 4th Infantry Division (22nd Infantry Regiment) and Technical Sergeant Edward Niland as an Army Air Force pilot in Burma, in the Pacific Theater.

Robert was killed on D day. His platoon had been surrounded and he manned his machine gun, harassing the Germans until the platoon broke through the encirclement. He had used up several boxes of ammunition before getting killed. He had also seen action in North Africa and Sicily.

Preston died the next day on Utah Beach and a third brother, Edward, was shot down and missing over Burma in the Pacific theater May 16, 1944.

Fritz Niland

Fritz, who had survived the first day was contacted through his Chaplain Francis L. Swanson and was notified of his brothers' deaths. Unlike Private Ryan there was no need to send out a rescue mission to find Sergeant Niland. Father Samson cleared the paper work necessary to send Fritz home and he was forced to return to the states, where he served as an MP for the rest of the war.

Fortunately for the Niland family, Air Force Pilot Edward Niland, had not been killed but had spent almost an entire year in a Japanese prisoner-of-war camp before being rescued by British forces. Robert and Preston are buried in the Normandy American Cemetery in France.

An interesting sidelight to all of this is that Fritz Niland married a lovely North Tonawanda girl, Marilyn Batt, whom I had dated before the war. Fritz and Marilyn have since passed away. I gathered much of this information from Fritz's cousins Joe and Jim Niland, who still reside in the Buffalo area.

Tom Niland, a cousin and close friend of Fritz's, was with the 101st Airborne Division in the battle of Bastogne, January 1945. He was shot in the arm while pinned down and knocked out a tank in this action. He was awarded a Purple Heart and the Silver Star for his heroism. He married, Phyllis Metzloff, whom I had taken to my senior high school prom. The Nilands had good taste.

Joe Niland, Tom's brother, was with the 20th Armored Division B Company. This division landed in Le Havre, France, February 18, 1945. They moved through France and Belgium to Aachen, Germany. They attacked and occupied Munich April 30. They then participated in the liberation of the Nazi concentration camp at Dachau, Germany. By mid-July, all units were en route to the USA with orders to Camp Cooke, California to prepare for the planned invasion of Japan.

After the war Joe and Tom continued their interests and participation in basketball. Joe eventually coached Canisius College in Buffalo and Tom was coach and then athletic director at LeMoyne College in Syracuse. They have a cousin, Art Belein, who also coached LeMoyne and is now head coach of basketball at West Virginia University.

The Niland family, in peace and war, is symbolic of the great traditions of competition on the courts, and dedication to the country on the battlefields.

College

College was a great experience for me. I went to the University of Vermont, primarily because my brother Jim had entered two years previously and was very fond of Vermont and his college experience. Jim was two years older and graduated in 1941. He had previously received a "first alternates" designation to the United States Naval Academy. Rather than wait for the first appointees to flunk the physical or be passed on for other reasons, Jim opted to take an athletic scholarship to the University of Vermont. He had been playing high school football for North Tonawanda, New York, under the coaching of Al Humphries. One of Al's college friends, Fuzzy Evans, was playing football at Illinois University. During their playing days

Fuzzy Evans

they had become very close friends and when Fuzzy went to the University of Vermont as freshman football coach he kept in touch with his old buddy Al.

About that time the University of Vermont was planning on an aggressive program to improve their football team. My brother Jim and one of his teammates, Norm Strassburg, then coached by Al, were offered scholarships to Vermont. After a visit to Burlington and being quite impressed by Vermont, Jim and Norm accepted scholarships to enroll at the University of Vermont.

Founded in 1791, UVM, which is an acronym for the Latin phrase *Universitas Verdis Montis'* or the University of the Green Mountains is the fifth oldest university in New England (after Harvard, Yale, Dartmouth and Brown) and among the 20 oldest institutions of higher learning in the country.

Kappa Sig Fraternity Classes of 1941 to 1944

Among its distinctions, UVM is one of the first universities to earn a chapter of Phi Beta Kappa, the honor society reserved for 15% of the country's most selective colleges, and in 1875 became the first to admit women into this society. The university pioneered in yet another epochal change of society, that of giving women equal status with men in higher education. In 1871, the university defied custom and admitted two women as students.

The campus of UVM is located in Burlington, the state's largest city with a population of 39,000, or of 140,00 in the greater Burlington area. It enjoys magnificent views of Lake Champlain, the Adirondack Mountains to the west and Vermont's Green Mountains to the east.

It was here that I began my college career. I took the course in engineering primarily because my brother was also an engineer. I actually aspired to a major in journalism, but this was not available at UVM at the time.

Jim and I along with about ten other athletes and aspiring athletes lived in a dorm we called "the Rock," located in the Rock of Ages business offices in Burlington. The dorm was on the third floor of an office building and we earned our room rent by cleaning the offices after the people went home. I had a job in a boarding house and some of the guys from the Rock also ate their meals there. I waited on tables for lunch and dinner so I could have free meals. Mrs. Moran was a great old Irish lady who ran the boarding house. She was in the early stages of cataracts and it was not uncommon to find a milk bottle cap in our chocolate pie. The other guys also had other jobs on campus as most of us worked our way through college.

My junior year in the fall of 1941 I was living at the Kappa Sigma fraternity house and my roommates were Clarence Akley and Harold "Misty" Rice. "Ake" was the steward at the house and gave me a job waiting on tables, so along with the other waiters I got free meals. Our cook was Eloise Magoon, a great gal from Stowe, Vermont. She did a wonderful job even in the midst of our many mashed-potato battles with the other waiters, including Bob Hennessey, a good friend of mine.

Misty Rice was captain of football and I was assistant manager of

The scullery crew at the Kappa Sig House: Bob Hennessey, me, and Don Maley

the team that year. Fuzzy Evans was football coach and had been my freshman basketball and baseball coach. At all of the football games one of my jobs was to sit next to Fuzzy and keep track of all the guys going in and out of the game. In those years, football players played both offense and defense.

Misty was a linebacker on defense and probably one of the hardest hitters to play at Vermont. He also played halfback on offense. In two of our major games that year, on the kickoff, he hit the receiver so hard he was out most of the game. Nobody played the game harder than he did. When the football season ended, we had racked up a less than successful one, winning two and losing six, although we did beat archrival Middlebury in the final game.

Football was over for the year; the Thanksgiving holiday had just passed and early in December 1941 everybody was getting ready for Christmas vacation.

On Sunday, the 7th, I was in my room at the Kappa Sig house doing some catch-up studying. I was also about to listen to the game between the Philadelphia Eagles and the Washington Redskins, when the broadcast was interrupted to announce that Japanese planes had launched a sneak attack on the American Naval Fleet in Pearl Harbor. In under two hours, Mitsuo Fuchida, pilot of the missions' leading bomber had accomplished his mission and the Japanese bombers were returning home.

They left the United States Armed Services to cope with 2,433 dead, 1,178 wounded, 18 warships sunk, and 188 planes destroyed – the worst day in American naval history. This infamous and cowardly attack suddenly changed our lives and we all realized that our next duties outside of college would be involved in the defense of our liberty. It was with this in mind that we went on that year at UVM.

The Southern Trip

The squad for the Southern Trip in 1942

During spring practice in 1942 we were all looking forward to the Southern Trip, an annual baseball route for Vermont when we usually played Army and Navy plus several other teams. The captain of our team, Johnny Spasyk, was a fixture at second base so I played in the outfield that year. One way to judge baseball players is as good field/no hit or good hit/no field; I was more of a no field/no hit ball player, nevertheless, I did make the team. Because the war forced cutting back on expenses and reduced supplies of gasoline, Coach Larry Gardner only took 13 men on the Southern Trip.

The traveling squad was as follows:

Clarence Akley, *pitcher. Throws right, bats left. Senior, Kappa Sigma. Lyndonville, Vt.*

Roy Alberghini, *pitcher. Throws left, bats left. Junior, Kappa Sigma. Orleans, Vt.*

Bill Benoit, *outfielder. Throws right, bats right. Junior, Phi Delta Theta. New London, Conn.*

Bob Carlson, *pitcher. Throws right, bats right. Senior, Delta Psi. South Ryegate, Vt.*

Tom Clairmont, *infielder. Throws right, bats right. Sophomore, Kappa Sigma. Burlington, Vt.*

Joe Corbett, *outfielder. Throws right, bats right. Junior, Kappa Sigma. North Tonawanda, New York.*

Bill Conrad, *catcher. Throws right, bats right. Senior, Independent, Morrisville, Vt.*

Joe Margolis, *catcher. Throws right, bats right. Sophomore, Phi Sigma Delta, Waterbury, Conn.*

Al Shaw, *pitcher. Throws right, bats right. Sophomore, Sigma Alpha Epsilon, Arlington, New Jersey.*

John Spasyk, *infielder, captain. Throws right, bats right. Senior, Phi Delta Theta, Pittsfield, Mass.*

Sig Sysko, *outfielder. Throws right, bats left. Senior, Sigma Nu, Bellows Falls, Vt.*

Russ West, *infielder. Throws right, bats right. Junior, Sigma Nu, Bridgewater, Vt.*

Hazen Wood, *infielder. Throws right, bats left. Senior, Delta Psi, Randolph, Vt.*

Fred Logan, *Manager. Senior, Phi Delta Theta, East Longmeadow, Mass.*

The University of Vermont 1942 Baseball team: 1st row– Conrad, Akley, Wood, Carlson, Coach Gardner, Sysko, Alberghini, Corbett, Clairmont; 2nd row– Pierce, Howe, Killick, Goldman, West, Cain, Mgr. Logan, Williams, Margolis, Bister, Carpenter, Blakely

The first game was against Navy and was a big thrill for all of us who had never made a Southern Trip. Just being on the Annapolis campus was a moving experience for all of us. They bunked us in the visiting team's dorm and we ate our meals in the large midshipmen mess hall. This in itself was a great experience, to rub elbows with all the navy midshipmen. There was a fair amount of the usual hazing as the plebes had to eat "Square Meals" and other of the usual freshman requirements.

The next day we played our first outdoor game of the year after having practiced in the dirt cage while the snow was falling in Vermont. Larry got us together before the game and gave his usual pep talk. He said, "Some of you new ballplayers might be a little bit nervous, but relax and don't worry, just play ball".

As usual Navy had a very good team. Phil Hurt was their pitcher and needless to say he more than hurt our batting abilities. I guess we got two hits off him and one hit off Lou Luberda his successor. Combined with eight big errors we suffered an 11-0 loss. So much for our Navy game. The Navy lineup was as follows:

Luberda, Hurt, *pitcher* / **Lavrakas**, **Syndersa**, *catcher* /
McNamara, *shortstop* / **Brennan**, *first base* / **Stowe**, *second base* /
Watson, **Rupert**, *third base* / **Cummings**, **Gillis**, **From**, *left field* /
Lacy, *center field* / **Schettino**, **Lasswella**, *right field*

Villanova was the next stop and we continued our hitting streak by going hitless against the Villanova team but beat them 2-1. After a couple of walks, an error and a sacrifice fly we scored two runs. Bob Carlson our pitcher gave up five hits and only one run.

Our next game we kind of redeemed ourselves playing Lehigh University at Bethlehem, Pennsylvania.

At Lehigh we looked up a Burlington friend of ours, Powell Whalen *(see page 206)*, who was a Sigma Nu fraternity member at Lehigh. Russ West, our shortstop, was a Sigma Nu'er at UVM, so Powell, as a good brother took us to his fraternity house for dinner and showed us around campus. Powell was a great guy and later a Marine hero in World War II.

We fortunately put on our hitting hats when we took on their baseball team that day and knocked out 17 hits to beat them 15-10.

Our final stop on the Southern Trip was to be against Army at West Point, New York. We really were no match for a hard-hitting Army baseball team as they breezed to an 8-2 win. I finally got an RBI by knocking Tommy Clairmont in with a single. The victory was the second straight for undefeated Army while we ended our trip with an even split in four games. The Army lineup was as follows:

Whitlow, *pitcher* / **White**, *catcher* / **Ford**, *shortstop* / **Corley**, *first base* / **Benson, Reinhalter**, *second base* / **Rickman**, *third base* / **Garland**, *left field* / **Mazur**, **Murphy**, *center field* / **Guckeyson**, *right field*

The real thrill of course was the beautiful West Point campus with all of its tradition and beautiful setting on the Hudson River. Then it was back to the Green Mountains and colder weather.

Larry Gardner – *Coach*

During my years in college I was able to enjoy a good mix of the usual college activities. I played some basketball, but my favorite sport was always baseball. Freshman baseball was a lot of fun and our coach was John "Fuzzy" Evans. My sophomore year I went out for varsity baseball. Larry Gardner, who had a great career with the Boston Red Sox, was head coach at the University of Vermont. Larry was one of the most unforgettable characters in my whole life. He was a father figure and a close buddy. As a coach he was relaxed and always gave you the impression of enjoying the game but never forgot winning. He fully participated in practices. One of the things I remember most was that Larry would always finish a hot shower with the coldest water possible before drying off. I always remember that during infield practice he would stand on home plate and hit "fungoes" to the catcher. These were fly balls straight up over home plate and were always difficult for the catcher. Even at a late age Larry was extremely versatile.

When Cobb's 24 year career ended, he said, "Larry Gardner was the best third baseman I ever played against." Larry knew that when Ty Cobb bit his lower lip at the plate, the great one was going to bunt, so he never bunted successfully for a base hit when Larry was at third.

The "Sultan of swat", Babe Ruth, echoed this sentiment about Gardner, his teammate with the Red Sox, and it was Cleveland writer Dean Snyder, who wrote in the early 20s:

> *American League pitchers would rather face Babe Ruth in a pinch than Larry Gardner. He is said to be the most dangerous man in either league at present when a hit will break up a ballgame or a difficult play will save the day.*

And after Gardner and Cleveland won the World Series in 1920 another writer typed:

He is probably, all things considered, the most efficient third base-man in the American League. He is a player of uncommon intelli-gence, good judgment and a credit to his profession.

Larry was a great storyteller. He would tell us many stories of his association with Babe Ruth and other famous Red Sox ballplayers. Some of these stories included the years when Babe Ruth was a great pitcher. Larry said that Babe Ruth was a big tobacco chewer. However, before each game the Babe would be pitching he would go over to Larry on third base and bum a big wad of Red Man or Mail Pouch from him before he threw his first pitch. He was generous but always bummed his "chews" from Larry. Babe still holds some pitching records with the Red Sox.

In the year 2000 Larry was inducted into the Red Sox Hall of Fame. This was a most well-deserved honor and something Larry never campaigned for, as he was a wonderfully humble man. He never wanted anyone to push him into the National Baseball Hall of Fame or Boston's own similar high honor.

Larry recalls that one year when they were playing the Yankees in New York, Babe was missing for one of the games. Larry and some of his friends knew that Babe had a friend over in New Jersey for a little extracurricular recreation. They went over to her apartment to pick Ruth up. His story relates that Babe would smoke a cigar after each romantic encounter. Larry said there were about eight cigar butts on the windowsill when they picked him up. Babe played hard on the field and off.

Following are the wartime experiences of the men who participated in the 1942 baseball trip.

Clarence V. Akley – *Pitcher*

Clarence Akley participated in ROTC at the University of Vermont, then graduated and received his commission as second lieutenant on May 18th, 1942.

From June 14th through September 8th at Fort Benning in Georgia he completed rifle and heavy weapons courses. He was then assigned to the Second Infantry Division, stationed at Fort Sam Houston, Texas. The division was moved to Camp McKay, Wisconsin, in November 1942, and remained there for training until September 28th, 1943, when the division was sent to Camp Shanks, New York for embarkation. His division went overseas on October 8, 1943, landing in North Ireland and remaining there until March 1944 when the division moved to South Wales.

The division landed in Normandy June 7, 1944. He was in command of the first machine gun platoon, Company M, Ninth Infantry Regiment. On June 24th while his battalion, the 3rd, was attacking the small town of Berigny, near St. Lo, he was hit in the back and foot by fragments of an 88 shell that struck a tree about 20 feet to his right. He was knocked unconscious by the blow and concussion. First aid men worked on him and when he regained consciousness a few minutes later, they carried him by stretcher to the battalion aid station, then by ambulance back to the 41st evacuation hospital near Trevieres. He received his first operation at this hospital 8 hours after he was hit. Then on June 27th, after receiving blood plasma and sugar to strengthen him, he was flown to England and spent one week at the 130th station hospital near Oxford, where his wounds were dressed daily. Penicillin shots and salt tablets were given to him every three hours from June 25th until July 20th.

Around July 3rd he was moved to the 186th general hospital north of Oxford. During the next four months he had four secondary closures on his back wounds, spending most of the four months lying on his stomach with pressure packs on his back.

In late October 1944 the wounds finally closed and he was up and walking around getting some strength back. On November 22nd he was sent back to the States, arriving at McGuire General Hospital, Virginia on December 3rd. Then he was shipped to Lowell General Hospital and received more treatments and massage until February

2, 1945, when he was released and sent back to Norwich University on temporary limited duty.

In October 1945 he was eligible for discharge on points and was sent back to Lowell General Hospital for disposition. They recommended permanent limited duty while awaiting the decision of the retirement board. He was then retired and separated on December 16, 1945. He went to law school at Harvard University, received his law degree, and retired to practice law in his hometown of Lyndonville, Vermont.

"Ake" had a successful law career although his back bothered him considerably through the remainder of his life. He passed away some time ago, with his peace and wartime distinctions as a legacy. He was a great roommate and friend to me in college and an excellent baseball pitcher for his alma mater.

Roy Alberghini – *Pitcher*

Roy Alberghini, a fraternity brother and teammate was a left-handed pitcher for the University of Vermont. I knew Roy ever since we were freshmen playing our first year at UVM. He graduated from UVM in May of 1943.

Upon graduation, he was drafted in July 1, 1943, and assigned to the Army Air Force, with basic training at Kiesler Field, Mississippi. He applied for and was accepted into the cadet training program qualifying as a navigator. He was sent to the Pan American School of navigation in Florida, graduating in July 1944, receiving his wings and the rank of second lieutenant. After overseas training he became part of the Eighth Air Force stationed at Tibenham, England. His first mission was to Düsseldorf, Germany, and he went on to fly a total of 26 combat missions over Germany. After the German surrender in 1945, he was sent back to the United States and discharged in October 1945. He received the European Theater ribbon with 3 stars and the DRC Air Medal with 3 Oak Leaf clusters.

He retired from the service and had a 33-year career teaching and coaching at Burlington, and South Burlington High School. He had a great life with his wife Connie, four sons, one daughter, nine grandchildren and two great-grandchildren. Roy died several years ago and I'll always remember him as a dear friend.

Bill Benoit – *Outfielder*

Bill Benoit was in my class at UVM and played football and base-ball. After graduation in 1943 he entered the Army Air Force and was a chief gunner on B-29 bombers. They were part of Curt LeMay's original 20th bomber Command stationed in Piardaka, India in 1944 and '45. In March 1945, the group moved to the Pacific and was stationed on Tinian Island in the Marianas. From that point they flew night missions over Japan until the end of the war.

Bill was discharged in November 1945 and arrived home in time for Thanksgiving. My wife and I have been friends of Bill and Helen for many years and still remain in touch.

Bob Carlson – *Pitcher*

Bob Carlson graduated from UVM as a second lieutenant in the quartermaster corps in 1942. He was stationed at Fort Frances in Cheyenne, Wyoming, and then ordered to Camp Lee, Virginia, to train recruits. He was range officer then company commander of a headquarters company, being promoted to lieutenant in '42 and captain in '43. In 1944 he was made an adjutant of a group at Camp Lee. In 1945 he was sent to Manila, Cebu, and Leyte in the Phillipines to train men on properly wearing protective clothing in cold, damp weather.

They were there when the Japanese surrendered and witnessed the thirteen Japanese coming to McArthur's headquarters. He was then assigned to the American division that went to Yokohama. There he was in charge of quartermaster companies scattered over a large area. In April 1946, having enough points for discharge, he returned to San Francisco and remained in the army reserve until retirement in 1974 as a major.

Tom Clairmont – *First Base*

Tom entered the service in 1942 at Fort Benning, Georgia, in Officers Training School. He had been in advanced ROTC at UVM and was a natural for officer training. After completing his training at Fort Benning, he was transferred to Fort McClellan for basic training in the anti-tank corps. He shipped out to Europe in 1943 and participated in the actions in Europe, the Ardennes, and central European campaigns.

Bill Conrad – *Catcher*

This information about Bill Conrad was sent to me by a friend of mine, Al Trepanier, who wrote as follows:

> *Regarding the information on Bill Conrad – he was wounded in the Philippines and was awarded the Distinguished Service Cross for valor. It is the second highest medal for valor. He returned back home for rest and recuperation. Rather than staying home, he returned to active duty.*
>
> *I was under very heavy fire in the town of Okie on Okinawa, and called for anti-tank cover. The unit that came was Bill Conrad's. The date was April 8th or 10th. He set up his unit when artillery fire opened up on us again. They had everything marked – one shell hit the tree above one of Bill's gun emplacements. The tree burst, killing Bill and members of his unit. I was also hit at that time and was flown to Guam Fleet Hospital 100. I returned May 30th and was wounded again on the 31st. So I had no further contact until I came home.*
>
> *Sincerely,*
> *Your friend, Al*

Al further suggested that I get in touch with Bill's commanding officer, Cliff Kimsey, who is currently living in Cornelia, Georgia. I contacted him and received the following letter:

> *It pleases me to be able to respond to your call seeking information about Bill Conrad. There is enclosed herewith a somewhat formal description of Bill's army activities. In a less formal manner, I would like to state that I could not have been more pleased to have been asso-*

ciated for about three years with Bill. His family background and mine were identical. His college experiences, including baseball, and mine were identical. In addition, Bill was probably a man of the highest character, morally, spiritually and professionally, that I encountered while in the army. What a shame that he could not have realized his potential in his world after the war.

You inquired about Al Trepanier. May I say simply, that he was the best soldier in the 32nd Infantry Regiment, and probably the best soldier in the Pacific Theater. Not only the best, but also the bravest (perhaps the dumbest). It is my memory that he holds five purple hearts and several other Distinguished Service Medals. I'm very pleased to say that he is still my friend, and that we stay in touch.

You are to be congratulated for your attempt to revive the memory of your college baseball teammates. I wish you success in that effort.

Respectfully,
Cliff Kimsey Jr.

Following is the information about Bill Conrad's service in the U.S. Army as outlined by his commanding officer.

ATTU / In April 19th 1943 the 32nd Infantry Regiment was part of a force that invaded Attu Island, during which Conrad's guns were used mostly for close support of the foot troops.

KWAJALEIN / In February 1944 the 32nd Infantry Regiment was part of a force that invaded Kwajalein Island. During this operation, Lieutenant Conrad directed the landing of troops and ammunition, weapons, water, food and other supplies during the entire operation.

ENIWETOK / Lt. Conrad commanding the first vehicle to hit the beach, after debarking the troops, remained on the beach giving machine-gun support to the landing. He noticed that the officer commanding the landing troops was still on the beach and had not urged his troops to get off the beach. Whereupon Lt. Conrad jumped out of his vehicle, proceeded to urge the troops to advance, and, in effect led the attack inland. While trying to neutralize a Japanese machine gun position, Lieutenant Conrad was seriously wounded, shot through the neck. For this heroic and voluntary action Lt. Conrad was awarded the Distinguished Service Cross. He was a long time recovering from the wound but was reassigned to the company just in time to be involved in the next operation of the regiment.

LEYTE / In September 1944 the 32nd Infantry Regiment was part of very large force that invaded the Philippine Islands. Lieutenant Conrad participated in this operation.

OKINAWA / On April 1st, 1945 the 32nd Infantry Regiment was an active unit in the initial invasion of Okinawa. This regiment was assigned an area that was on the left flank of the Seventh Division area; the First Battalion on the regiment's left flank. Lt. Conrad's guns were positioned with the left-most company because that terrain, being on the coastal plain, was the only area conducive to tank operations. Late in the evening, Lieutenant Conrad had called his squad leaders together to discuss the plans for the attack the following morning. Only one enemy artillery round was fired, but it happened to get the gun that was the closest to the meeting spot. Lieutenant Conrad was fatally struck by a large piece of shrapnel from that round.

Fred Logan – *Manager*

Fred Logan was the manager of our team and became a close friend of all the guys. Immediately after graduation Fred enlisted in the Marine Corps parachute troops. While he was in training he and several other Marine Corps friends of mine were passing through New York and looked me up at diving school. Anxious to have a night on the town, a girl I knew got Fred and his other friend a blind date. Fred's' date was a nice girl named Mary Lou and during that date Fred and Mary Lou got along beautifully. To make a long story short they eventually married and had a beautifully successful marriage.

After visiting me Fred rejoined his paramarine unit. The following year, along with many other Marines, he was shipped to the South Pacific. On October 1st, 1943, while participating in the battle of Vella Lavella, Fred was wounded and awarded the Purple Heart. He stayed in the Marine reserves retiring as a major. From then till the present I have kept in touch with Fred who is living in Florida. He is another one of the truly outstanding friends I had on that baseball team.

Joseph Margolis – *Catcher*

Joe Margolis from Waterbury, Connecticut, was the catcher for our team. Soon after he graduated he enlisted in the army and soon was in the Pacific Theater. He participated in the battles of the Ryukyu Islands, that began on March 26,1945, and lasted till July 2nd of that year.

During the battle for Okinawa (one of the Ryukyu chain) on May 21, 1945, Private Joe Margolis was killed in action.

Albert Shaw – *Pitcher*

Al – or "ambidextrous Al" as we called him because he could pitch either left-handed or right-handed – naturally pitched right-handed, although he was just as wild either way. Al graduated from UVM and immediately reported to Fort Benning, Georgia, where he received his commission as a second lieutenant. He then went to the ordnance training center at Camp Santa Anita, Arcadia, California. From there he was transferred to the Philippines and New Guinea, serving as an adjutant to the colonel, and rose to the rank of captain in the infantry. He was stationed in that area until war's end when he returned to the States.

John Spasyk – *Second Base*

Johnny Spasyk was one of the best athletes at UVM. He played quarterback on the football team and was a great second baseman on the baseball team. He wasn't very big, but pound for pound was one of the best athletes I've ever known.

Johnny majored in ROTC military in college and graduated as a second lieutenant. He went into the service in the spring of 1942 and was in the 103rd Infantry Division. This division soon went to Europe and his outfit participated in many actions in France, Germany and Austria. After leaving the service he stayed in the Army Reserve until January 1967. He retired as a lieutenant colonel, taught school, and became a principal. He passed away in September of 1982 and is buried in Arlington cemetery.

Sygmund Sysko — *Center Field*

Siggy was our best hitter and a great center fielder, always hitting in the clutch and playing flawless outfield. He was an engineering student and when he got out of college enlisted with a commission as lieutenant. He was advised at that time to continue his engineering studies as the recruiters on campus said engineers were urgently needed in industry. The Philco Corporation hired him as they were manufacturing radar equipment, bombsights, proximity fuses, and other devices needed by the military. He was involved in the design of signal receiving radar devices installed in B-17 and B-24 long-range bombers used over Europe. This was all top-secret work and these individuals received frequent deferments to implement these very important projects. Siggy was with Philco for 32 years, contributing to their vital involvement in the war effort and other engineering work throughout his career.

Russ West — *Shortstop*

Russ and I first became friends when we went out for freshman baseball our first year in college. I was the second baseman, and Russ played third. We also played freshman basketball and knew each other well. I will always remember our freshman basketball team — we both spent some time on the bench. One of my most memorable games was when we were playing Green Mountain Junior College. It was a close game and our prospects of playing were minimal. There were vendors selling ice cream bars to the spectators in the stands so I bought a couple that Russ and I shared on the bench. Needless to say, Coach Fuzzy Evans really blew his stack when he looked down the bench and saw Russ and me eating Eskimo Pies. I think we won the game but somehow or other I was scoreless.

When we were on the southern baseball trip, we played Lehigh University. Russ looked up a fraternity brother, Powell Whalen *(see page 206)*, who was then taking petroleum engineering. We knew Powell from Burlington and he took us to dinner at the Sigma Nu house. That was the last I saw of Powell until I met him in Burlington in 1951. He was then showing the effects of his tragic World War II wounds in the Marine Corps .

Russ volunteered for the U.S. Army Air Force in 1943 and soon after reporting was reassigned to the 28th Infantry Regiment. After training in Camp Croft they landed on Utah Beach July 4, 1944. An interesting episode occurred during this period. A fox terrier that was in his foxhole gave birth to a litter of five – somewhat of a rarity in the middle of a battle. Russ kept one of them all through the rest of his service, eventually bringing him back to the States. While in action at St. Lo, he and his dog were wounded and hospitalized. Russ claims that they both got Purple hearts.

After recovering from his wounds he was assigned to a reconnaissance group in the Tenth Armored Division. Later while participating in a mission overlooking Garmisch-Partenkirchen in the Bavarian Alps, Russ reported what happened:

Observing the town, that appeared to have been vacated, they recognized what appeared to be the focal point, the town hall. Mindful of the dangers of land mines and booby traps Russ assigned young Private Edgar Gentile of Pittsford, Massachusetts, to stealthily approach this building and ascertain the situation. They watched this 5' 3" soldier slowly advance and enter the building. About a half hour later out the front door of the hall appeared two German generals with their hands up followed by the diminutive doughboy with his pistol. These guys had been waiting for the U.S. army to show up so they could surrender.

Russ spent the rest of the war with a team deactivating mines and booby traps. He also played third base with an Army baseball team comprised of many professional ballplayers, that won the Third Army championship. He returned to the States with his faithful dog, married his college sweetheart Peggy Durfee, and now is retired to a farm in Vermont. He earned the Purple Heart, Silver Star, Combat Infantry Badge and the European Theater ribbon with four stars.

Hazen Wood – *Third Base*

After graduation in May of 1942, "Woody" went directly into the United States Army as a second lieutenant in the 28th Infantry Division, stationed at Camp Livingston, Louisiana, General Omar Bradley commanding – this by way of Burlington, Vermont so he could marry Janet Rust, his college sweetheart.

Right after their wedding they went by Pullman car to St. Louis, changed to a troop train loaded with soldiers being called back on duty to go on maneuvers with the 28th. Woody left on maneuvers two days after they arrived in Virginia – some honeymoon to begin a marriage.

After four months the 28th was sent to Camp Carrabelle, Florida for ship-to-shore training. Four months later they moved to Camp Pickett, Virginia. By then, Commanding General Bradley had been promoted and given a fifth star.

In September of 1943 the division was sent to Wales where they trained for the invasion. However on June 2nd they were sent to London on leave, as a diversionary tactic because the Axis "knew" that they were training for D-Day. They went to France soon after D-Day. Known as the "Bloody Bucket" division, they landed on Normandy beaches July 22nd, and by the 31st they were in the thick hedgerow fighting. August 20th found them rolling eastward along the highways of France. An advance north to the Seine trapped the remnants of the German Seventh Army, capturing Vernuil, Breteuil, Le Neuberg, and Elbuf as the count of prisoners mounted.

On the 29th of August the division entered Paris and paraded under battle conditions before a populous delirious with joy. There was no time for rest, however, and the advance continued onward, and on the sixth of September they crossed the Meuse River.

After receiving a Purple Heart, Hazen returned home in 1945 and was discharged from the army. He had a successful career as a teacher and then joined the faculty of UVM College of Education for 10 years. In 1984 he was recognized as an Outstanding Educator by the New England Association of School Superintendents. "Woody" has since passed away and has left a legend of great accomplishment on the baseball field, the battlegrounds of Europe, and in higher education.

The Navy and Army Games

The two games against Navy and Army were contests between a bunch of guys from the University of Vermont pitted against a select group of America's finest. We were all engaged in a friendly rivalry of many years as Annapolis and West Point had been scheduled regularly on the Vermont southern trip. My brother Jim had participated in these games as a UVM's catcher in 1939.

In the spring of 1942, baseball was the big deal in our lives and whether we got hits and runs or made errors defined our concerns. As we competed with the service teams none of us knew what the future might hold after graduation. Within the next year these same players were actively participating in their contribution to the war effort. In many cases some of the guys had lost their lives or were wounded, serving our country all over the world.

The World War II war records of the players significantly shows the many ways in which we served our country.

The Players: United States Naval Academy Baseball Team in World War II

Warren J. McNamara – *Shortstop*

Upon graduation Warren was commissioned an Ensign June 9, 1943. On August 9, 1943, he was transferred to the USS *Doran DD 634*. This ship performed escort and patrol duties between Bizerte, Tunisia and Sicilian ports, and other duty between New York and the United Kingdom. On October 10, 1943, Ensign McNamara was lost overboard during heavy weather while making an inspection tour of the ship. The *Doran* received three battle stars for World War II service.

William S. Luberda – *Pitcher*

William Luberda received his commission after graduating from the Naval Academy in 1942. During World War II he served aboard the light cruiser USS *Birmingham* and participated in the invasion of Sicily and in the invasion of Saipan. After attending flight school at Corpus Christi, Texas, in 1944 and 1945, he was attached to a fighter squadron in Coronado, California, until 1947. He served with the Atlantic Fleet Air Command and was executive officer aboard the aircraft carrier *Bennington* from 1953 to 1954. He served as air officer aboard the carrier USS *Valley Forge CVS-45*, in the Atlantic, Mediterranean, and Caribbean in the late 1950s. The *Valley Forge* won the Battle Efficiency Pennant in 1959. He was head of the component and accessory branch of the Bureau of Weapons and retired in 1964 with the rank of commander.

John Joseph Brennan – *First Base*

John Brennan served aboard the USS *Birmingham CL-62* from October 1942 to December of 1944. The *Birmingham* after her shakedown cruise joined the Atlantic Fleet in June 1943. She steamed to the Mediterranean and gave gunfire support during the invasion of

Sicily in July of 1943. In August of 1943 she was reassigned to the Pacific Fleet and arrived in Pearl Harbor on September 6th, 1943. Joining the fast carrier task force screen, she took part in the raids on Tarawa and Wake Island. At the Solomons she took part in the action during which she destroyed the Japanese plane that hit her with two bombs and a torpedo. After repairs at Mare Island she rejoined the Pacific Fleet in February 1944. She took part in the invasions of Saipan, Tinian, and Guam and the Battle of the Philippine Sea. She then served with taskforce 38 during the Okinawa, northern Luzon, and Formosa raids and the battle for Leyte Gulf. During the Leyte Gulf action she suffered topside damage from explosions on board *Princeton CVL-23* while courageously attempting to aid that stricken vessel. After Lieutenant Commander Brennan left the ship in December 1944 the *Birmingham* supported the invasions of Iwo Jima and Okinawa. On May 4th, 1945, after fighting off three attacks the Birmingham was damaged for a third time when a Japanese suicide plane hit her forward. She then returned to Pearl Harbor for repairs. The *Birmingham* received nine battle stars for her World War II service.

Lefteris Lavrakas – *Catcher*

After graduation in 1942 Ensign Lavrakas served aboard the destroyer USS *Eberie DD 430* as gunnery officer in the Mediterranean, participating in the actions during the North African and Anzio campaigns. From September 1944 through October 1945, he was the gunnery officer on the USS *Aaron Ward* participating in the Okinawa campaigns when she was hit by six kamikaze planes. Rising to the rank of lieutenant he served on the USS *Mansfield* from November 1945 to July of 1947 as the executive officer and navigator during the occupations of China and Japan in 1946 and 1947. He commanded the Royal Marine and South Korean task elements on 16 separate operations against North Korea in 1951 and 1952. In World War II one year he earned the Asiatic Pacific campaign ribbon with one star and the European

Theater with two stars. He had further outstanding service in the Navy, retiring in 1970 with the rank of captain.

Arthur Gillis – *Left Field*

During World War II Ensign Gillis served on the destroyer USS *Sproston DD 577* as a torpedo officer and then executive officer. He participated in the raids on Kurile Island in early 1944, Leata campaign, Battle of Leyte Gulf, the recapture of Subic Bay, and the Okinawa campaign. He earned the American Defense Medal with one star, the Asiatic Pacific with four stars, the Victory Medal, the Philippine Liberation with two stars, and later the Korean campaign ribbon.

George Watson – *Third Base*

Ensign Watson graduated from the Naval Academy in 1943 and was assigned to the USS *Frazier DD 607* as first lieutenant serving in the Asiatic Pacific Theater, where he earned three Bronze Stars. In October 1945 he entered flight training school and graduated from Pensacola Naval Station in aviator advance training.

Jack Stowe – *Second Base Captain*

Upon graduation Ensign Stowe served on the USS *Kendrick DD 612* a newly commissioned destroyer. After a shakedown period she was ordered to the Mediterranean where she participated in the landing at Scoglitti, Italy. Later, while acting as escort for a convoy of transports and aircraft carriers, the convoy was attacked by enemy aircraft, the *Kendrick* was badly damaged by a torpedo hit. After serving on the *Kendrick* he attended flight training school and was designated a naval aviator, serving consecutively with bomber fighting squadron 82 and fighting squadron 18-A. After his career in the Navy he retired in July 1988.

Frank Schettino – *Right Field*

Upon being commissioned in June of 1943 he was assigned to the USS *Gansevoort DD 608* and participated in World War II combat operations in the Gilbert, Marshall, and Philippine islands. In 1946 he was operations and gunnery officer on the staff of the commander, destroyer squadron 15, whose operations were patrol and occupation duties off Japan and China. He participated in the Korean conflict in 1950-1952. His many awards included Asiatic-Pacific Campaign (two stars), Korean Service Medal (four stars), Phillipine Liberation Medal (two stars), and Korean Presidential Unit Citation and Bronze Star Medal with Combat V.

Walter Rupert – *Third Base*

After Walter Rupert's commissioning in June of 1942 he reported to the USS *Long* for duty. He had other temporary duties in Washington and Norfolk and was in 1944 ordered to the USS *Drexler DD 741* that was being fitted out in Bath, Maine. The USS *Drexler* was later involved in enemy action in the Asiatic Area. Lieutenant Rupert was killed in action on May 28th when the *DD 741* was lost.

Paul L. Lacy Jr. – *Center Field*

Following graduation from the Naval Academy in 1942 Paul Lacy joined the USS *Cleveland CL 55* and, while on board that cruiser, saw action during the North African invasion and in operations at Rennel, New Georgia, and Bougainville Islands in the South Pacific. He is entitled to the Navy Unit Commendation awarded to the USS *Cleveland* for outstanding action during the battle of Empress Augusta Bay in November 1, 1943. In 1944 as gunnery officer on the USS *Sea Cat SS 399* he received a Navy Commendation Medal, "For distinguishing himself as torpedo data computer operator in a United States submarine during a war patrol of that vessel."

In subsequent years after 1946 he was the executive officer on the USS *Paya SS318* and later became Division Engineer on the staff of Commander Submarine Division 51. He next joined the USS

Entemedor SS 340 to serve as executive officer and then commanding officer. In 1954 he was in command of the USS *Guitarro* SS 363 that was reconditioned and loaned to the Turkish Navy. For the next two years he commanded the USS *Pickerel SS 524.* After further nuclear propulsion training he was assigned to the USS *Ethan Allen SSBN 608* and assumed command of that fleet ballistic missile submarine upon her commissioning in 1961. "For meritorious achievement" while commanding the Blue Crew of that submarine he was awarded a gold star in lieu of a second Navy commendation Medal. In 1965 he was deputy director of the Special Projects office, Office of Naval Material, Navy Department.

Following selection to the rank of Rear Admiral in 1966 he became Commander, U.S. Naval Support Activity, Danang, Republic of Vietnam in February 1967, that time being the Navy's largest over-seas shore activity. "For exceptionally meritorious service," while at Danang he was awarded the Distinguished Service Medal. In 1968 he was Commander Amphibious Group Three in the western Pacific and as Commander Amphibious Force, Seventh Fleet supporting military operations in Vietnam. For performance of duty in this assignment he was awarded the Legion of Merit with combat V. He was later involved in the Navy's efforts to construct the newest class of high-speed attack submarines. In 1970 he assumed command of the U.S. Pacific Fleet submarine force, and for "his distinguished performance of duty" in that capacity, was awarded a gold star in lieu of the Second Legion of Merit. He served in that capacity until reporting in November 1972 as Deputy Chief of Naval Material. On October 1, 1973 he was transferred to the retired list of the U.S. Navy.

The Players: United States Military Academy Baseball Team in World War II

Henry Joseph Mazur – *Center Field, Captain*

Henry Mazur graduated and was commissioned a second lieu-tenant in January 1943. While a cadet at West Point he trained as a fighter pilot at Stewart Air Force Base, earning his Silver wings before graduating from the academy. During his years at West Point he was captain of football and an All-American choice in 1942. After flight training he went to England with the 396 FS and flew 83 aerial missions encompassing some 224 hours of combat flying time. He participated in air offenses in Normandy, Northern France, Rhineland, and the Ardennes-Alsace. He also participated in the famous Berlin airlift. Among his many decorations, commendations, and awards he was presented with the Distinguished Flying Cross with Oak Leaf cluster from the Ninth Air Force, the Air Medal with 16 Oak Leaf clusters and the Air Force Commendation Medal. He was a veteran of World War II, Korea, and Vietnam and had 26 years of active service for his country.

John William Guckeyson – *Right Field*

After his graduation from West Point in 1942, Bill was sent to Moore Field, Texas where he received his wings and was sent over-seas in December of that year. Captain Guckeyson quickly became a flight leader in a P-47 Thunderbolt Squadron and was assigned as bomber escort on raids over Europe. In the spring of 1944 he experienced his fifth victory in enemy engagements. Two of his first four had resulted from air engagements and two involved destroying planes on the ground. For his fifth victory Captain Guckeyson was flying at 20,000 ft. when he spotted a twin-engine Junkers 88 far below. He and his wing man spiraled down onto its tail and shot the bomber down for his fifth kill.

On an air mission to Stendel on May 21, 1944, his plane was shot down and he was seen parachuting to earth. However, reports were never confirmed and he was declared lost. A fellow pilot in the squadron wrote to his wife in 1945, "He was about the most regular and most capable pilot in the 361st Fighter Group and that's no exaggeration. I know for fact that he often led the whole squadron. His photo was in a prominent place in the pilot's room and was one of the largest ones. Everyone looked up to him."

Another friend wrote, "He took all his imitation of the God of 'compassion and love' when he flew out in his shiny new P-51 for his last run on May 21, 1944. We will remember no one in our Class with deeper regard, affection, and joy."

Bill was 28 years old.

John Carter Ford – *Shortstop*

After graduation Johnny went to flight training school at Kelley Field, Texas. He was awarded pilot wings in December 1942 and trained for P-38 fighter aircraft. He was stationed in England in January 1944 with the Eighth Air Force. He was promoted to captain on January 17, 1944, and twice awarded the Distinguished Flying Cross. Johnny died at Honington, England on July 8, 1944 in an air accident. He was flying a P-38 that had just had an engine change. On takeoff the aircraft suffered engine failure; the plane flipped over and crashed upside-down a few miles from the Huntington runway. Thus a tragic accident ended the career of a brave young Air Corps officer. He loved his country; he showed valor in combat; he gave his life.

Joseph W. Benson – *Second Base*

Joseph Benson graduated from the U.S. Military Academy in 1943. He was a veteran of more than 12 years in the Army having served in Europe and in the Far East. He is the holder of the Bronze Star Medal and the Commendation Ribbon, and retired as a colonel in 1963.

William C. Garland – *Left Field*

William Garland Wright graduated from the U.S. Military Academy in May of 1942. He completed pilot training and received his pilot's wings in March 1943 and B-17 training in April of 1943. During World War II he served with the 401st Bombardment Group stationed in England and flew 32 combat missions in B-17 bomber aircraft. His decorations and service awards are as follows; the Distinguished Service Medal, Legion of Merit, Distinguished Flying Cross with Oak Leaf cluster, Air Medal with three Oak Leaf clusters, Air Force Commendation Medal with two Oak Leaf clusters, Army Commendation Medal, Distinguished Unit citation emblem with one Oak Leaf cluster, Air Force Outstanding Unit Award Ribbon, European African Campaign Medal with seven service stars, World War II Victory Medal, National Defense Service Medal with one star, Air Force Longevity Service Ribbon with five Oak Leaf clusters, and the croix de guerre with bronze star from France.

During postwar years he rose to the rank of major general in January 1969. General Garland served as staff officer for SAC, commanded a SAC bomb squadron, and graduated from the Air Command and Staff College. After a tour at SAC headquarters the general went to Madrid and became Chief of Staff for the Joint U.S. Military Group and later served with the 16th Air Force in Spain. He served in command positions for SAC and had a tour with the office of the Secretary of the Air Force. In August 1969 he was Commander of the 1st Strategic Aerospace Division, Vandenberg AFB.

Edgar Allan Rickman – *Third Base*

Ed Rickman served as a company commander and battalion executive officer in the 307 Infantry 77th Division in the Pacific Theater. The 77th Division participated in the actions on Ie Shima and Okinawa. During the fighting on Ie Shima the well-known war correspondent Ernie Pyle was killed and later buried in the 77th Division cemetery there. Lieutenant-Colonel Rickman received two Bronze Star Medals and two Purple Hearts.

Robert Victor Whitlow – *Pitcher*

Bob Whitlow was one of the Army's best athletes, lettering in football, baseball and basketball. In January 1943 he was among the 170 members of his class to graduate with pilot's wings. He entered combat in December 1943 in the European Theater and flew B-24 Liberators as aircraft commander and operations officer in the 458th bomb group. Along with several other West Point graduates with bomber experience they formed the Eighth Air Force Scouting Force.

Flying P-51 Mustangs ahead of the bomber forces, they served as scouts for weather, enemy flak, and enemy fighters. On one mission Bob and his fellow pilots saved a B-24 group by shooting down numerous German fighter planes and disrupting their attack. Bob flew 550 combat hours in one bomber tour and three fighter tours. He destroyed eight enemy aircraft including two FW-190s in flight. He received the Silver Star, four Distinguished Flying Crosses, and eight Air Medals.

Active in athletics after the war, he became the first director of athletics and head football coach when the United States Air Force Academy was founded in 1954. He retired from the Air Force as a colonel and later became General Manager for the Chicago Cubs. Following his baseball work he formed the Phoenix Roadrunners, a Western Hockey League franchise. He passed away in July of 1997. His accomplishments and his life pay tribute to the motto of the United States Military Academy, "Duty, Honor and Country."

Ernest Johnson White – *Catcher*

After graduation in May of 1942 Ernie went into flight training and received his wings in December 1943. After a short stint in P-43's he was assigned in the spring of 1943 as a P-47 Thunderbolt flight commander in the 359th fighter group. In August 1943, the group sailed to England and was stationed at Martlesham Heath, near Ipswich. In the course of flying 128 combat missions and shooting down four German aircraft, Ernie successfully moved through the ranks – from flight commander, to 359th fighter squadron operations officer, squadron commander, and finally as deputy director of operations for the eighth fighter command, where he was promoted to lieutenant colonel. During the Korean War he commanded the 4,000 men who fought as the 502nd tactical control group. In the Vietnam War he was in a command position at an air base in Thailand.

His decorations included the Legion of Merit, distinguished Flying Cross with two Oak Leaf Clusters, Air Medal with ten Oak Leaf Clusters and the Korean Military Order of Merit, that nation's second highest decoration. He had many other assignments in the air force, was a professor at Miami University and with the committee of the National Security Council in Washington D.C. In 1970 he was promoted to Brigadier General, capping off a splendid career in the military. He passed away in March of 1988.

John Richard Murphy – *Center Field*

After graduation John was commissioned in the infantry and went to flight training. Upon receiving his wings and assignment as a fighter pilot, John knew early on that flying was his thing. He liked nothing better and became one of the best. During World War II John served with the fifth air force in the European Theater, first as a pilot and then as Commander, 388th Fighter Squadron. He became deputy commander of the 365th Fighter Group and in March 1945 assumed command of the 40th Fighter Group as a lieutenant colonel. By the end of World War II, John had flown 139 missions totaling 305 combat hours in the P-47 aircraft and was awarded the Silver Star, two Distinguished Flying Crosses, and 31 air medals. During the Korean War he flew 30 combat missions in the F-51 fighter aircraft. Upon reassignment to the 49th fighter group, he led the group on 89 missions in F-80 aircraft. He again distinguished himself in combat and was awarded three more Distinguished Flying Crosses, the Legion of Merit, and eight more air medals. In 1965 he was sent to South Vietnam and was Deputy

Commander, 2nd Air Division 13th Air Force. He was back in combat for the third time. In 1973 he was promoted to Lieutenant General and was Deputy Commander in chief, United Nations Command in Korea. He retired in 1975. As a patriot, leader, teacher, diplomat, and fighter pilot he served his country with the utmost of courage and distinction. He died in January 2000.

William Edward Corley – *First Base*

William Corley was with an antiaircraft artillery group in the European Theater of operations during 1943-45. He was awarded two Bronze Stars during this period. He later served in Berlin and Turkey with a military assistance advisory group, at NORAD headquarters, American War College, and was Executive Officer of the 52nd Antiaircraft Artillery Brigade. He received the Legion of Merit in 1968 and retired as a colonel in 1969.

Other University of Vermont Friends in World War II

James H. Tennien – *Pittsford, Vermont*

Jim and I first met in 1939 when we enrolled in the mechanical engineering course at UVM. We became close friends and frequently studied together as we took the same courses. He was a brilliant engineer and greatly helped me get through college. We quite often skied and studied together. Several Thanksgivings, Jim invited me for dinner on their farm in Pittsford. In January of 1943 we graduated, and as an engineer and an ROTC student he went into the army to be a lieutenant in the U.S. Air Corps. His first assignment was to Wright Field, Ohio, to work on and test-fly top-secret radar equipment. One night while testing radar in a P-38 plane he crashed and was killed. Jim was my first very close friend to give his life in the service of his country. It was a real shock and I will never forget him.

My son Joe lives in Jim's hometown of Pittsford, Vermont, and I recently visited him on Memorial Day, May 28, 2002. My triplet grandchildren, Joe, John, and Jim, and their younger brother Jeff were with the Cub Scouts in the town parade, that ended at the church library and town cemetery. Joe's wife Jean had worked in the library and knew that Jim Tennien had been buried in the Pittsford cemetery. After the parade she arranged for us to visit his grave site. It was a beautiful summer day as we walked through the cemetery and located his grave adorned with newly placed American flag. To our great surprise Jim's younger brother Tony, and his older sister Mary had been making their Memorial Day visit to

their brother's grave. After introducing myself and relating the history of my friendship with Jim I shook hands with Tony, and gave Mary a big kiss. It was a Memorial Day occasion that I will always cherish. I took a picture of Jim's headstone and we slowly walked back to the car.

George Edward Little – *Burlington, Vermont*

George Little (left) and me in 1941

"Spook", (I never knew where he got that name) and I were in the same class at UVM except he was in the Arts College and I was a lowly engineer. We were both members of the Gold Key and Boulder honor societies and through mutual friends got to know each other very well. We all took ROTC together and George enlisted in the Army Air Corps in July of 1942 and went on active duty in January of 1943. He had his basic training at Camp Lee, Virginia and his Air Force flight control training at Orlando, Florida. He went overseas in November 1943 to New Guinea with the 56th Fighter Control Squadron. He participated in operations in New Guinea, Morotai Island, and the Philippines. He had as much sea duty as some Navy guys serving as a fighter director on the USS *Stevens DD 479*, the *Smith DD 378* and the *Blueridge*. They were involved in the Philippine landings and the Borneo operations. He directed air defense of army bases in New Guinea, Netherlands, East Indies, and the Philippines. The destroyer duty involved voice-over radio, coordination of antiaircraft, Infantry and Navy and utilization of radar. George received the Adriatic Pacific Service Medal with four battle stars and one Bronze Arrow, the Philippine Liberation Medal with one Bronze Star, the World War II Victory Medal and campaigns: New Guinea, Luzon, Southern Philippines, and Ground Combat Borneo.

George and I have been close friends since 1939 and in 1950 became partners in the George Little Press from which we retired in 1986. We still see a lot of each other.

Howard C. Vreeland – *Rutherford, New Jersey*

Howie was a mechanical engineer in my class and graduated in January of 1943. We were close friends during our college years and in the summer of 1942 we both worked for our meals at the De Goesbriand Hospital. Right after graduation he went on active duty as a corporal at Fort Devens, Massachusetts, moving on to Fort Monmouth OCS Signal Corps training, and then commissioned a second lieutenant in May 1943. He then commenced combat training and radio school and after further training went to the signal depot in Lexington, Kentucky. From the Olmstead Air Base in Harrisburg he reported for embarkation in Boston on November 23, 1943, arriving in England December 17, 1943. In August of 1944 his unit went to the staging area at South Hampton. He was made S-3 Supply Officer of the 3159th Signal Service Battalion readying supplies for the battalion to go to France. They landed at Utah Beach September 3, 1944, and then entered Rennes, Normandy, until Jan 5, 1945. Howie then went to Paris to activate a new battalion, the 3,160th Signal Service Battalion. After serving in France and the Rhineland their battalion on July 22, 1945, sailed from Marseilles, France, via the Panama Canal to Manila, arriving August 28th, 1945. Howie had been on active duty and had only 9 days leave to get married to a college sweetheart, Lyn Eimer, in 1943.

While his battalion was in Manila about 75 percent of them contracted dysentery and were in the 80th General Hospital for some time. On November 15, 1945, they embarked on an LST for Yokohama, Japan. On January 10, 1946, Howie got his orders back to the States, sailing on an APA to Seattle. Arriving on Jan 29, 1946, then to Fort Dix and separation on Feb 6, 1946. He had accumulated 79 days of terminal leave after active duty of three years and four months. He earned the American Campaign Medal, an Asiatic Pacific Campaign, European and African, Middle Eastern, Phillipine Liberation and World War II Victory Medal. We have been in close contact all these years and see a lot of each other.

John J. White – *Needham, Massachusetts*

John "Whizzer" White was a fraternity brother and lived at the "Rock" where my brother and I lived my freshman year. He played baseball and varsity football and, like a lot of Boston guys, also played hockey – but in those days UVM didn't have a hockey team. He graduated from UVM in 1942 and immediately went into the service on May 22nd. He was soon sent to the European Theater and became part of the enlisted men of the 78th Infantry Division. He later was a Platoon Sergeant of the Regimental Mine Platoon 309th Infantry Regiment. He went into combat December 11, 1944 in Hürtgen Forest just south of Aachen, Germany, and north of Malmédy. During these actions he was wounded. Returning to the States he was discharged on November 5, 1945. He received the European Theater ribbon with stars, Combat Infantry Badge, Purple Heart, and the Bronze Star.

After the war he was a certified public accountant and practiced in Brewster, Massachusetts. The last time I saw Whizzer was at his 60th reunion several years ago at UVM when we reminisced on our college days. He recently passed away at the age of 86 leaving three daughters, his brother Bob, a sister and two granddaughters. I will always remember him as a fraternity brother and a courageous competitor on the gridiron as well as on the battlefield.

Robert F. White – *Needham, Massachusetts*

Bob White was John White's younger brother and graduated in the class of 1944 at UVM. He enrolled in the U.S. Naval Officers' Training School at Northwestern University and received his commission. He was sent to the Seventh Amphibious Force serving on the USS *Ancona* as a gunfire liaison officer. He went ashore with the infantry during seven landings in the Pacific Theater and earned the Silver Star and the Bronze Star.

Bob practices law in the Boston area and has been on the Board of Trustees at Lawrence Academy for many years.

Captain Robert Hennessey (right) receiving the Distinguished Flying Cross Medal

Robert E. Hennessey – *Bridgeport, Connecticut*

Bob was a Kappa Sigma in the class of 1943. We were close friends all during college and worked together waiting on tables at the fraternity house. He was famous for his active participation in mashed potato fights in the kitchen, much to the chagrin of Eloise, our cook. He enlisted in the Air Corps July 24, 1942, and went on active duty November 19, 1943. He was with the 15th Air Force 97th Bomb Group in Foggia, Italy. He sent a summary of his experiences:

"I flew 33 missions as a Radar Mickey operator navigator, bombardier in B-17s. Radar was relatively new at this time as an aid to navigation to see through cloud formations and locate targets. Thus the radar-equipped planes were always in the lead of the group. My first 10 missions were so difficult I thought I'd never reach the 35 necessary to return to the States. The war ended when I had 33. I was then sent back to the states to train in B-29s for Pacific duty. The Japs capitulated and that was the end of that."

Bob earned the Distinguished Flying Cross, the Air Medal with 30 Leaf clusters, and the European Theater Ribbon with four battle stars.

He returned to Bridgeport after the war and went into the undertaking business. After selling it to his competitor, he has been clipping coupons ever since. I still hear from Bob and his beloved Peggy quite often.

Richard Healy – *Lynbrook, New York*

Dick Healy was in my brother Jim's class of 1941. He was also a fraternity brother and excelled in baseball and basketball at UVM. In his senior year he was the head steward and ran the table at the Kappa Sigma house. He gave me a job waiting on tables so I was able to get free chow.

After graduation in 1941 he was drafted in February of 1942. He went through basic training at Camp Croft, South Carolina, after that he was recommended for flight school in the Air Corps. Failing the eye exam for flight training, he was assigned to the physical education unit and helped with recreation programs. During this period he met Hank Greenberg, the ex-Detroit Tiger first baseman, who recommended he apply for an administrative position in the Air Corps. Graduating with a commission as second lieutenant, he became an airplane recognition instructor and transferred to Brooklee Field in Alabama. After a tour of duty there, he was sent to Camp Custer in Michigan to attend Provost Marshal general school. Following another assignment at Brooklee Field that unit was later disbanded he was sent overseas in January 1944. They spent 33 days on a Liberty ship in the biggest convoy of the war. After landing in Naples, Italy, he was transferred to Brindisi with the 566th Air Service Squadron and became the adjutant. This squadron was sent to Foggia, Italy, where B-17 bombers were flown in from England and serviced by that unit. In June of 1945 he was made a captain and transferred to the 531st Service Squadron as their supply officer. After having spent two years in Italy he was rotated home and discharged on April 28th 1946. He had spent 4 years and 2 months in the service. Dick married his college sweetheart Marge Whitham February 16, 1946. They have seven children and 15 grandchildren and reside in Westborough, Massachusetts. Dick returned to the

University of Vermont several years ago, and I attended the ceremony when he became a member of the University of Vermont Athletic Hall of Fame.

William Roeder – *Queens Village, New York*

Bill Roeder was in the class of 1943 at the University of Vermont. He was a member of the SAE fraternity, and we became close friends through several of my other buddies who were also SAEs. He was a real sports fan and was the Sports Editor of the *Cynic*, the University's weekly newspaper. He was one of those guys unfortunate enough to be classified 4F and be deprived of the opportunity to serve his country. In his army physical he was diagnosed with a heart murmur that precluded any opportunity for him to enter the service. This was a great disappointment to him as he was destined to play out the war as a civilian. In 1943, when I was in diving school at Pier 88, Bill frequently socialized with me and some of my Navy friends. It was always obvious that he felt uncomfortable not being in uniform.

During the war and in the late 40's he became one of New York's premier sports writers. While a columnist with the *World Telegram* he traveled with the Brooklyn Dodgers reporting all their games. During those years after the war while I was working in Detroit I was fortunate enough to visit Bill on the Dodger's trips to Chicago, Pittsburgh, and other cities where they were playing. I always stayed with Bill in his hotel room and it was frequently a gathering place for all those great Dodgers of that era. Bill was well liked by all of the players and it was a great thrill for me to meet Peewee Reese, Duke Snyder, Gene Hermanski, Cookie Lavagetto, Pete Rieser, and many of the other ballplayers. Oddly enough one of my high-school classmates – Stan Rojek, an infielder – was also on the squad. These were wonderful days for me as a baseball fan to meet so many of the great "Boys of Summer." Bill lived Dodgers and wrote Dodgers. In 1950 he wrote *Jackie Robinson,* still considered the first and most definitive book on Robinson.

Bill later became a senior writer for *Newsweek* – he wrote the

"Newsmakers" and later the "Periscope" sections. In August of 1982 during a reunion at his lake cottage with old sportswriters from the *World Telegram*, he suffered a heart attack and passed away. He will always be remembered as one of my friends who was greatly disappointed that he hadn't worn a uniform in the service of his country, through no fault of his own.

We are still in touch with his widow, Eileen, and exchange Christmas cards every year.

Ralph LaPointe – *Winooski, Vermont*

Ralph was a member of the Class of 1945 at UVM and also a Kappa Sigma fraternity brother. As a freshman he starred in football, baseball, and basketball. He was an excellent athlete but showed his most promise in baseball. Like most of us he worked hard during college, earning extra money to pay for tuition and other college expenses. I recall Ralph and his wife, Kit, made sandwiches and sold them to all the fraternity houses on the hill. When he would come to the Kappa Sig house, he would come up to my room and invariably manage to slip me a free sandwich. In my senior year I was manager of the football team, and Ralph and I often roomed together on football trips. In the fall of 1942 Ralph with several other of my friends entered the Enlisted Reserve Corps, which allowed them to continue one more semester at UVM. In January of 1943, this group (including my close college friend, George Little) was sent to Fort Devens, Massachusetts, for their basic army training. Ralph was an excellent student, could speak fluent French, and ultimately was enrolled in the American Special Training Program (ASTP) at Haverford College to study Italian.

His next tour of duty was at Camp Ritchie, Maryland, where he was the athletic and recreation director. During his stay at Camp Ritchie he played baseball for the Frederick, Maryland team under the assumed name of Joe Moss to keep his amateur standing.

At war's end and after his discharge he worked on a State Department program in Mali, Africa, in a recreation program teaching the fundamentals of basketball to the natives.

During 1947 and 1948 he played major league baseball with the Philadelphia Phillies and the St. Louis Cardinals. He was on the All Rookie National League Team in 1947. Ralph returned to the University of Vermont and in 1952 succeeded Larry Gardner as varsity baseball coach. He was a charter member of the UVM Hall of Fame and was a popular and successful coach until 1968 when he passed away.

Norman K. Strassburg – *Essex Junction, Vermont*

Norm Strassburg was from my hometown of North Tonawanda, New York. He played football in high school with my brother Jim and they both came to the University of Vermont on scholarships. They were in the class of 1941.

After graduation in 1941 Norm volunteered for the U.S. Coast Guard and entered the service on August 20, 1942. He was assigned as a physical trainer for recruits at the Norfolk Naval Base with the rank of Boatswains Mate 1st Class. Seven months later he was assigned to the newly launched frigate, USS *Gladwoyne PF 62,* as a boatswains mate. He was also assigned as the gun captain of #1, 3-inch cannon on the ship. They did a lot of convoy duty from Boston and Norfolk Naval Bases to the North Atlantic, Iceland, and the Mediterranean Sea with a home base in Oran, North Africa. He was also assigned to the diving panel on a captured German U-boat. He returned to the States and was discharged on September 28, 1945. He received the Good Conduct Ribbon, the European and African Middle Eastern Campaign Ribbon, and the American Campaign Ribbon.

After the war Norm returned to his home in Essex Junction, Vermont, and married his college sweetheart Kay LeBaron. He joined the staff of the University of Vermont Athletic Department on which he served until his retirement.

Everett Bailey – *Burlington, Vermont*

I first got to know Everett Bailey when I was a freshman in ROTC. He was an upperclassman in advanced military ROTC at UVM. These were the guys who had finished their basic two years of mandatory military training and had opted to continue the next two years in advanced military. Ev was active in the ski program and was captain of the ski team in his senior year. Graduating with an electrical engineering degree, he held a civilian job right out of college. Pearl Harbor changed all our plans and in January of 1942 he entered the service.

The Army had activated its first mountain unit, the 87th Mountain Infantry Battalion, at Fort Lewis, Washington, on December 8, 1941.

Everett Bailey and "Bounce" at Fort Lewis, Washington in 1942. *"We were good friends. I stayed on post weekends to ride out with Sgt. Strait, Stable Sergeant. I was Executive Officer D Co. 87th 1st Br. reinforced, that later expanded to the 10th Mountain Division. We had horses and mules, a blacksmith shop and saddlery tent in our corrals – and a sign on the corral gate – 'Through this portal pass the most beautiful mules in the world.' I had charge of the horses and corrals. I hated to leave the job, but Father Brachen talked me into becoming adjunct for Dick Reily C.O. of newly formed 2nd Br. Then when we left Fort Lewis for Kiska I had to bid goodbye to Bounce."*

They trained on Mount Rainier, Washington, a 14,408 foot peak. This was Ev's first unit as the National Ski Patrol was recruiting skiers for the 87th.

Ev became company commander of 87-F, and in the summer of 1943 they were shipped to the Aleutian Islands for the Kiska operation against the Japanese. The Japanese, however, after losing Attu in May of 1943, had decided to evacuate Kiska. Toward the end of July 1943 and shrouded by fog, two light cruisers and ten destroyers worked their way into Kiska Harbor and removed the 5,100 men of the garrison in a few hours.

Unaware of the Japanese evacuation, on August 16, 1943, American and Canadian troops assaulted Kiska. All that remained were Japanese mines and booby traps.

The 87th soon returned to Camp Hale, Colorado, to be part of a new organization known as the 10th Light Division (Alpine). The combat power of the division was contained in the 85th, 86th, and 87th Infantry Regiments. On July 19, 1944, he joined company L of the 86th at the request of the battalion commander John Hay and took command on July 21st. The division's year training at the 9,200-foot high Camp Hale honed the skills of its soldiers to fight and survive under the most brutal mountain conditions.

On November 6, 1944, the 10th Division was redesignated the 10th Mountain Division.

On December 10, 1944, the division embarked on the SS *Argentina* from Hampton Roads and after 13 days at sea arrived in Naples, Italy. On December 26 they embarked on the Italian freighter *Sesteire* for Leghorn and to Pisa to prepare for combat.

The division entered combat on January 28, 1945, in the North Apennine Mountains of Italy. They faced German positions along the five-mile long Monte-Belvedere Ridge. Other divisions had attempted to assault Monte-Belvedere three times, even holding it temporarily but none had succeeded. They first had to take Riva Ridge, that protected the approaches to Monte-Belvedere. A surprise attack scaling the 1,500-foot vertical ascent took the ridge on

February 18, 1945. The Monte-Belvedere assault was next.

It was heavily manned and protected with mine fields. Everett's L Company was selected for the flanking attack mission and performed remarkably well in spite of heavy casualties, including all platoon leaders. L Company captured the division's immediate objective, called Massancana. A day or two later Ev provided a task force to fill a defensive gap in the battalion defensive line on the next hill. That force was most effective in the destruction of a German counterattack and captured many prisoners. In the final battle the Third Battalion captured Torbole. He was extremely proud of his company. General Truscott told Ev and Battalion Commander John Hay that the 10th was the best division on the Gothic Line and northward.

On April 14, 1945, the final phases of the war in Italy began. The 10th Mountain Division attacked toward the Po Valley spearheading the Fifth Army drive. The fighting was fierce with the loss of 553 mountain infantrymen killed, wounded, or missing on the first day. The final combat for the 10th Division took place in the vicinity of Lake Garda. On April 27, 1945, the first troops reached the south end of the lake, cutting off the German army's main escape route to the Brenner Pass. Using amphibious DUKWs they bypassed the destroyed tunnels and roadblocks and captured the towns of Riva and Torbole at the head of the lake. Organized resistance in Italy ended on May 2, 1945.

The 10th Division completely destroyed five elite German divisions. In 114 days of combat, the division suffered casualties of 992 killed in action and 4,154 wounded.

After a period of occupation Everett flew back to the States in advance of the division's return for a 30-day leave. The 10th Mountain Division was to be used in the projected invasion of Japan. These plans ended with the surrender of Japan on August 14,1945. Shortly after the Japanese surrender he was discharged in late August of 1945. After the war he was in the reserve as a commanding officer of the second battalion, 304th Infantry, 76th Division. He taught in the commanding General Staff College, was Aide to the

"Hit th' dirt, boys!"

"Wot's funny about horizontal foxholes?"

When I think of my friends who slogged through the mud and scaled the mountains up through Italy and into the Po Valley, I recall the characters of Willie and Joe, created by Bill Mauldin. Mauldin began his career in the 45th Infantry Division as a private in company K, 180th Infantry Regiment. These cartoons appeared in *Stars and Stripes* that circulated among the servicemen during World War II. They were about the ordinary guys doing their job in circumstances ranging from merely awful to truly appalling. Without them, no wars could have ever been won. These were typical of my friends who were in the 10th Mountain Division. Bill Mauldin and Ernie Pyle epitomized the correspondents who dug down and got dirty with the enlisted men and reported from the trenches as well as the command posts. Here are three cartoons showing Willie and Joe, who lent a touch of comic relief to the grim reality of the war.

"Joe, yestiddy ya saved my life an' I swore I'd pay ya back. Here's my last pair of dry socks."

Secretary of the Army, retired in 1965 with the rank of colonel. He was awarded the Combat Infantry Medal, the Bronze Star twice, and the Silver Star.

The following citation for the Bronze Star was awarded to Everett on March 23, 1945. It reads as follows :

Everett C. Bailey, 0-389133, Captain, Infantry, United States Army. For meritorious service in combat February 20, 1945, near Mt. Gorgolesco, Italy.

When his company's scheduled advance upon a major objective was halted by heavy enemy fire,the fearless conduct and keen tactical knowledge displayed by Captain Bailey rallied and inspired his men with new determination and vigor to drive forward. Continually moving about, many times under fierce enemy fire, he directed effective fire and led well planned movements that enabled the completion of his company's mission with a minimum of casualties. Such a superior performance of duty merits much praise and gains the respect of all who know of it. Entered the military service from Burlington, Vermont.

By command of Major General George P. Hayes.

The following citation was made to Captain Bailey on July 22,1945.

Under the provisions of army regulations 600 -45, as amended, a Silver Star medal is awarded to the following named officer:

Everett C. Bailey,0-389133, Captain, Infantry, 86th Mountain Infantry, United States Army. For gallantry in action on 19 and 30 April 1945, near Monte Giorgio and Torbole, Italy. When the leading company of a battalion,attacking a strongly defended ridge,was halted by intense enemy resistance, supported by tanks, Captain Bailey moved his support company forward and led the way for other battalion elements in the final assault. When one of his platoons was pinned down by fierce fighting from hostile strong points in buildings, and entrenchments, he personally led the attack on one of the enemy emplacements, killing many of the enemy and capturing several prisoners. Without slowing the assault, he directed the attack and capture of several other strong points and quickly secured the hotly contested ridge. In a later battle when casualties had depleted the battalion staff, he took command of the battalion and directed its operation in a courageous and efficient manner. During a strong enemy counterattack supported by armor, he made his way through artillery and small arms fire to direct the maneuvers of his forward elements in repulsing the hostile attack. His superlative leadership, gallant conduct under fire, and outstanding military skill greatly assisted his battalion in the winning of every objective, and have earned for him the highest praise. Captain Bailey's heroic deeds are truly in keeping with the finest traditions of the United States Army. Entered military service from Burlington, Vermont.

Leon H. Baker, Captain, Infantry Records Custodian.

He married Doris Doerfler in Morrisville, Vermont on January 17, 1943. They have four children and four grandchildren. Everett and I have maintained our friendship for the many years since we left the service. We play golf together three times a week. Our several foursomes include Francis Cain, former Mayor of Burlington, John Cain former Probate Judge of Chittenden County, Phil Hoff former governor of Vermont who became the first Democrat to be elected governor serving three terms, and John Carpenter and Proc Page. At this stage in our lives we're not hitting the ball as far as we used to – and being 80, not shooting 80 – hearing aids, golf carts, and bifocals are an essential part of our equipment. We do have fun with our usual one dollar Nassaus and friendly matches. Sometimes over a beer or two we might even reminisce about our years in the service. These precious friendships make our fading years a real joy.

Harold "Red" Crossley – *Gardner, Massachusetts*

When my brother Jim was a freshman at the University of Vermont in 1937, he was on the freshman football team. One of his closest friends on that team was "Red" Crossley, a Gardner High-School and Cushing Academy quarterback. They became great friends and I recall Jim writing home and telling about the new friends he had on the University of Vermont freshman football team. He especially mentioned Harold Crossley, who was quarterbacking their freshman team. Jim was invited down to Red's home in Gardner and met the Crossley family. Red excelled on that team and as sophomores the following year Jim and he were on the varsity football team at UVM. Sadly enough that year Red injured his knee and his future football career ended.

Right after Pearl Harbor Red enlisted in the Air Corps, trained as a fighter pilot, and early on went into combat in Germany.

Jim Corbett, Dick McDonough and Harold "Red" Crossley in ROTC

Red's history as a fighter pilot is memorialized at the Millville, New Jersey, Army Airfield Museum. In this museum the leather flight jacket of Captain Harold "Red" Crossley hangs next to a plaque honoring his memory that reads as follows:

> *Crossley, a Gardner High and Cushing Academy star athlete, was a World War II fighter pilot who flew over 60 combat missions, shot down four German aircraft, won the Distinguished Flying Cross Medal, and lost his life in a training mission in New Jersey on April 2nd, 1944.*

Mike Stowe of Millville, New Jersey, who researched the record of Crossley said, "Captain Crossley was a man who had hundreds and hundreds of Germans perfectly willing to end his life at any time, and he managed to cheat them. And yet he came back to the United States and lost his life in an accident. It was really a bizarre twist to a time of war. Of the 14 men killed at Millville, only Captain Crossley had combat experience. He was there as an instructor. For him, the war was over. He had served his time, he was back in the States."

Stowe knew the specifics of Crossley's death. "He was leading a flight of training pilots and developed a fire in flight. His plane was burning and he bailed out successfully, but he was badly burned and drowned in very cold water about 10 miles offshore."

Blanche Holmlund, Red's sister, remembers that April day in 1944 when her family received the tragic news. "My mother just sat in the chair and rocked. She couldn't say anything."

Red was married only six months before he died. He was 26 years old. I knew him as a member of our fraternity when I was a freshman and will always remember him as one of my brother Jim's best friends.

Paul Edward Corley – *Burlington, Vermont*

Paul Corley was in the class of 1941 with my brother Jim. He was an excellent basketball player and also a Kappa Sigma fraternity brother. I got to know Paul very well during my freshman and sophomore years. He graduated in 1941, volunteered for the Army Air Corps and went on active duty in December 5, 1943. He trained as a B-17 bomber pilot and, as a 2nd lieutenant was stationed in England in 1944. On September 11, 1944, during a bombing mission over Germany he and his crew were shot down. He was rescued and held as a prisoner of war for 10 months in a prison camp in Barth, Germany. During his stay in the prison camp he met a mutual friend of ours, John Cain from Burlington, who had been captured after parachuting safely when his plane was shot down.

One of the first persons John ran into when he arrived in the prison camp was Paul Corley, who offered him a cigarette.

Paul remained in the prison camp for about 10 months and when the Russians liberated them he was airlifted by the Eighth Air Force to Belgium. He arrived back in the United States in June of 1945 and was discharged October 1, 1945.

After his service career he returned to Burlington, went to medical school, and became a radiologist. He practiced in New Bedford, Massachusetts, for more than 30 years and retired in 1987. We visited Paul and Peggy, his wife, several times. He passed away in 1994 leaving a fine family of two sons and three daughters.

Donald W. Maley – *Great Barrington, Massachusetts*

Don Maley went to the University of Vermont and was a classmate of my brother's in the Class of 1941. He was also a fraternity brother, and like some of us worked for his room and board at the fraternity house. He was in charge of the Coke and candy machines. This was a nice little side job and got a few extra bucks for Don. When he graduated he gave me the keys to the machines and told me to take over. No big deal about selling the business or anything, he just gave it to me.

He was a very good basketball player and also made the varsity in football and baseball. In recent years he was elected to the University of Vermont Athletic Hall of Fame.

Upon graduation in 1941 he did some coaching of high school basketball and in March of 1943 was drafted into the army.

On May 12, 1943, the Americans assaulted Attu and the Japanese were cleared out by the 28th of May. Don's outfit was part of the occupation forces that took over Attu and prepared for the invasion of Kiska. On the 16th of August in 1943 American and Canadian troops assaulted Kiska but it wasn't until several days later that they realized the Japanese had been totally evacuated. Some time after that Don was sent to Officers Candidate School at Fort Lee in Richmond, Virginia. He received his commission as a second lieutenant and about that time the war ended. In May of 1946 he was discharged and returned to Burlington, Vermont to continue an illustrious basketball coaching and teaching career. He and wife Rita Mahoney raised a fine family of five boys and four girls. I coached his son Marty, who could hit the long ball just like his dad, in Little League Baseball.

Edwin Joseph O'Connell – *Springfield Massachusetts*

Eddie O'Connell and I first met when we were freshmen at the University of Vermont in September 1939. We were both taking the same courses in mechanical engineering. I joined the Kappa Sigma fraternity and Eddie was an SAE, but we both saw a lot of each other in class. He was on the track team and the football squad and I played baseball and freshman basketball. When Pearl Harbor happened in 1941 our engineering class was accelerated and we continued classes through the summer of 1942, graduating in January of 1943. On that cold day in January Eddie was the marshal of our class. A year earlier when the Navy recruiters came to campus he signed up for a program called "Aviation Volunteer Probationaries" and was commissioned an ensign in April 2, 1942. In February after graduation he reported to MIT to take a full course in aircraft engine design. His second assignment was to Norfolk, Virginia to study aircraft maintenance. From Norfolk he was sent to Ream Field in California to train for a carrier aircraft service unit named CASU #17. He was next assigned to Ford Island, Hawaii, as a squadron engineer for SBD Navy planes.

Eddie was anxious to get more involved in the war effort and was assigned to *CASU #22* and in February of 1944 they were sent on the invasions of Eniwetok Atoll. After the Marine landings the Seabees built an airstrip and Eddies unit set up the power stations to provide lights and power for the air group.

A new outfit came to Eniwetok called SCOFA. This was Shipping Control Officer Forward Area. Their mission was to keep track of all the ships in the Pacific area. They assigned shipping routes for merchant ships going to the Pacific areas, Australia, and back to the states. They would also brief warplanes as to merchant ship locations and where our own submarines were operating. He constructed a large map on a four by eight plywood board where they could keep track of the various groups of the ships in the Pacific. While on this assignment he met Admiral King on his visit to Eniwetok

In July of 1945 Eddie returned to the states for his first leave after two years. While back in Boston visiting his college sweetheart and fiancee, Katherine Hayes, the war ended. His last assignment was as transportation officer in San Diego, California. Discharged from the service in San Diego on May 16, 1946, he received the Pacific Theater Ribbon with two Battle Stars, Good Conduct Medal, and a recommendation from Admiral John Hoover for the regular Navy.

We saw a lot of each other after the war when we were both working in Rochester, New York. He subsequently was employed with the Bechtel Corporation and rose to Vice-President in charge of sales in the power division. Former Secretary of State George Schultz was a top executive with Eddie here.

Eddie and Kay lived in La Quinta, California. Eddie was an avid golfer. They lived on the La Quinta golf course and he played virtually every day. He quite often would play in the Bob Hope golf tournament and on several occasions asked Mae and me to visit them during this annual affair. One year in particular when we went out he asked me to drive his golf cart during the tournament. Being that this was a famous celebrity invitational tournament, his partners included the movie great Jack Lemmon and pro golfer Lanny Wadkins. Needless to say we had a wonderful time as Jack Lemmon proved to be one of the finest and most delightful men I had ever met. We had lots of laughs and Eddie and his partners also played some fine golf. The O'Connells visited us quite often as Kay's mother still lived in Burlington. Sadly Kay passed away in 1994.

I still see Eddie and his new wife Shirley and we saw each other at our 60th college reunion in June of 2003.

Harold "Misty" E. Rice – *North Haven, Connecticut*

Misty Rice was one of my roommates my junior year at UVM, in the class of 1942. Before actual graduation, he volunteered for the Marine Corps, hoping to become a pilot and finally joined the paratroops. As a member of the First Paratroop Battalion he participated in some rough combat at Bougainville and Vella Lavella. They were also part of the occupation forces at Guadalcanal. In January 1944 the paramarines were disbanded and the men used to help form the Fifth Marine Division. Misty went back to the states and married his college sweetheart Harriet Woods. Another one of my friends and a fraternity brother, Larry Killick, also a Marine, was the best man at their wedding.

Shortly after that, it was back to Hawaii and the formation of the Fifth Marine Division. On his previous visit to Hawaii after Bougainville he had gotten in touch with my brother Jim who was with a CASU unit at Hilo. They had played football together at the University of Vermont and were also great friends. Jim naturally was glad to see him and made a great effort to treat him royally at his quarters in Hilo. The Fifth Division was at Camp Tarawa near Kamuela, a small village next to the Kohala Mountains on the big island of Hawaii. They were training for the invasion of "Island X," which turned out to be Iwo Jima. The staging area for Iwo was Saipan and from there it would be a three-day cruise to Iwo.

Following in his own words is Misty's description of D-Day on February 19, 1945:

D–Day

The mission of the 28th Marines was to land on Green Beach and capture Mount Suribachi, a strategic fortress. Our First Battalion led the assault on the extreme left flank. Baker was to the extreme left and Charlie Company was to its right. The company orders were to drive across the island and cut it in two, thus isolating Surabachi and dividing the Japanese forces. Able company was in reserve. The Second and Third Battalions were to come in behind the First Battalion and assault Mount Surabachi itself. The Second Battalion, 27th Marines was on Charlie Company's immediate right. It was to head north and assist in taking the first airfield.

Upon landing it was an effort to walk and almost impossible to run in the sandy soil with all our gear and equipment. On the second or third terrace I ran into the first casualty who was hit 3 or 4 times with machine-gun fire. I tried to console him, placed him in the best position I could and told him to wait for help as bleeding did not appear to be a factor. I made several attempts to contact the command post personnel or anyone who might answer their radio but to no avail – nothing but static and mixed chatter. I never did see our CO Phil Roach and it wasn't until we proceeded farther that we came upon Lt. Wes Bates, all alone, wounded himself, directing and encouraging individuals and groups forward. He had already reached the west shore, our objective, and was on his way back, when he was hit by machine gun fire fracturing his left arm. I didn't have any idea of what time it was at that point but it was still early, probably between 1030 and 1100 hours.

Our group, I'm not sure how many, continued the assault as we realized this was a "must" invasion and time was of the essence. About midway across the island I was hit myself. A bullet entered the base of my neck between two vertebrae and came out on the left side of my neck. It was not a serious wound, but it knocked me down and stunned me. After being patched up I returned alone to the west shore where our company, Charlie, was preparing their defenses. It was a great feeling to see our troops and to know we achieved our objective. However, we had to hold on to what we achieved. We spent the rest of the day clearing and flushing out the enemy on all sides around us. We wanted to consolidate and defend our positions, that were still very vulnerable, before nightfall. We were expecting infiltrations and possibly an all-out attack that night. An attack did start and the Navy did pick it up. A destroyer offshore spotted a barge full of troops, and let go a star shell that illuminated the whole area where we were overlooking the shoreline and the entire beach. We caught them dead in their tracks and had a field day. It was later reported that the boatload of troops had come up the west shore from Mount Surabachi. The Navy continued the use of star shells when needed throughout the operation. They were most helpful. As the day ended Mount Surabachi was isolated and I had a very positive feeling that first night."

D+1 Feb. 20, 1945

On the morning of the second day the three battalions of the 28th Marines, Fifth Marine Division, occupied a line across the neck of the island facing southward toward Surabachi. The attacking force for the second day consisted of the Second Battalion on the left and the Third battalion to their left. The First Battalion was in reserve. Its mission to mop up behind the lines.

Artillery, naval gunfire, and air strikes for the attack on Suribachi began soon after daybreak. The attacking forces began their attack at 0830 hours. As soon as they started the Japanese responded with constant barrages of heavy and small arms fire that instantly slowed our *attacking forces. The problem was one of direct observation by the enemy on Mount Suribachi and the lack of concealment for our troops. C company continued mopping up operations. All the platoons had areas to cover behind the lines. Lieutenant Wes Bates was still with us in spite of a broken arm sustained during the fight to cross the island. His performance in leading the attacks on major fortifications was outstanding. As a matter of fact the whole company was on top of this situation and did everything possible to help. We did lose people during the mop-up period. One was Gunner Mowery, our Company Gunnery Sergeant. He went with a patrol to protect and guide a vehicle across the island. It was the first shipment of ammo and supplies to be delivered to the west shore. Japanese surfaced along the way, and threw several grenades with one exploding in front of the gunner. He sustained multiple wounds of the chest and abdomen and had to be evacuated.*

Very little progress was made against Mount Suribachi the second day. At night heavy guns and mortar continued from both sides. Star shells and our mortars kept complete darkness at bay. Generally we occupied the same positions we had the first night. There was one difference. It rained and we were soaked, not having all the gear we started with.

D+2 Feb. 21, 1945

The attack on Mount Suribachi would continue this third day with the Second Battalion, on the left, Third battalion in the center, and one company from the First Battalion on the right (west side). The pre-attack bombardment ended with a 40 plane attack against Suribachi's base. Those on the beaches, east and west, simply rose and started walking toward Suribachi's' flanks. Opposition in the center was still strong. Behind the lines the covering artillery continued firing and the battle raged. Tank support was implemented and at midday the Second Battalion reached the base. The Third Battalion had not reached the volcano but were not far out. The flanking companies along the east and west beaches moved around the volcano's flanks without any opposition. Charlie Company continued mopping up operations and except for heavy artillery and mortar fire, also naval gunfire, conditions were improving, and we could move about more freely.

On this third night 25 kamikaze aircraft from Japan went after Turner's invasion fleet off Iwo. Thousands of tracer bullets of all sizes filled up the sky from the fleet in the immediate area. The Japs managed to bomb or ram five vessels. The worst two were aircraft carriers. The Saratoga suffered more than 300 killed and wounded, and was so badly damaged it had to head for Pearl Harbor. The Bismarck Sea swept by fire, exploded and sank, with a crew loss of over 200 men. Not one pilot survived.

D+3 Feb. 22, 1945.

This morning about three battalions of the 28th Marines prepared to tighten their grip on Suribachi's base. As it turned out, it was pretty much of a mop-up operation. The network of caves around the base still had many live Japanese but they were completely surrounded.

C Company was still in the process of mopping up behind the front when we got our orders late in the afternoon to fill a gap between B company on the left and the water on the west shore. We completed the job just as it got dark. Several infiltrators attempted to get through that night with no great success. I assume they were killed or wounded.

D+4 Feb. 23, 1945

This was flag raising day. Elements of the three battalions who were not already there, moved forward to the base of Suribachi. There was no opposition in Charlie Company area and little in any of the other sections. We merely walked to the base of the volcano and along the west side. It was not climbable at that point. C company 23rd Marines controlled the only route up the mountain and they had the honor of raising the flag.

It's ironic, but our company couldn't see the flag from our vantage point. When we left this area on D+9 I don't remember the flag because I was involved in getting our troops up to the north end of the island. Regardless, it was a booster!

D+9 Feb. 28, 1945

On the 10th day we prepared to replace CT27 at Hill 362 A. Reports had it that the 27th had a rough time and that they were pushed back off the hill. We would move out under cover of darkness to the area near 362 A and prepare to take the hill. We moved out *single file through the night and were in our new positions on the first slope of the hill before dawn. Charlie Company was on the right flank of the First Battalion with Companies A and B on our left flank. The Second Battalion 23rd was on A company's flank with the third Battalion 28th on their left moving up to the beach, all in a northerly direction. Elements of the Third Division were on C Company's immediate right. We started off soon after it became light trying to maintain contact with our adjacent units. During this action we lost several key people through sniper fire. The biggest blow, however, was the artillery barrage that hit in our Company Command Post area. We were never sure of how many we lost from that one shelling. We have had estimates of between 10 to 20. The sad thing is that some who were there thought it might have been friendly fire. That could have happened, as artillery that day was active on both sides of the line. We continued our advance and late in the day surged forward and beyond Hill 362 A on our right flank. That night nothing moved and it was quiet in our sector.*

Shortly after the Iwo operation Misty was ordered back to the States for discharge. He was transported on an escort carrier back to San Diego, California, where he was subsequently discharged from the Marines, ready to go back to civilian life. Misty Rice had made his contribution to the defense of his country with the same all-out effort and sacrifice as he had displayed on the football field and throughout his life. During his Marine career he was awarded the Asiatic area ribbon with stars and a Purple Heart.

Harold "Misty" Rice at his UVM Hall of Fame induction with Larry Killick (right) and myself (left)

We have been in close touch all these years and gotten together in Florida and at our respective homes. Two years ago Misty came back to Burlington and the University of Vermont when he was inducted into the UVM

Athletic Hall of Fame. Also in attendance was Larry Killick, another Marine and a close friend of ours who was also a Hall of Famer.

Just before these memoirs were to be printed I received a phone call from Misty's daughter Carol informing me that he had passed away on July 5th. He had been in declining health for the past few years and this wonderful guy had finally attained the ultimate Hall of Fame. We had all lost a great friend. The memories of Misty Rice on the gridiron and as a fighting marine will be with us forever. We will miss him.

Lawrence Findlay Killick – *Burlington, Vermont*

Larry Killick and I first met in 1941 when I was a sophomore at UVM and he was a freshman. Larry was a Burlington native and an outstanding basketball and baseball player at Burlington High School. He pledged the Kappa Sigma fraternity of which I had been a member since my freshman year. During these years Larry and I became close friends. I graduated in January of 1943 and Larry, while still in college, volunteered for the Marine Corps and enrolled in the V12 program at Dartmouth College. There, Larry played varsity basketball under the tutelage of Earl Brown. He was on the first team and starred that year when Dartmouth lost only one game and ranked number 2 nationally. In that graduating class were two other Burlington natives, Jack Shearer and William Muir. I knew Billy Muir from Burlington. We met again when Bill was the catcher on the Bowdoin College baseball team that we played during the 1942 season in Maine.

After two semesters at Dartmouth, his first duty was at Parris Island, South Carolina. In that boot camp training class there were more than 75 outstanding athletes who had gained fame in the annals of their respective intercollegiate sports. Parris Island is the source that creates the most disciplined, dedicated, and professionally competent military organization of its kind in the world. After this first indoctrination in the Officer Candidate Program they were next sent to Camp Lejeune in North Carolina. This was the epitome of physical training, and only a Marine who has experienced it could describe the rigors of this chapter in their training

Quantico was the fourth phase of Larry's Marine training. On arriving he found out that another close college buddy of his, and friend of mine, Tony Lewkowicz, was in the OCS class ahead. About 10 days after Larry arrived at Quantico, he returned to the barracks one evening to find out that Tony had been killed that afternoon in a mortar fire training accident. This devastated him as it was the first loss of one of his V12 buddies and a dear friend.

In August 1944 Larry graduated and was commissioned a second lieutenant in the United States Marine Corps. The next step was Camp Pendleton, Oceanside, California, to prepare for the ultimate assignment to the Asiatic Pacific Theater. In early January they boarded the troopship USS *General Hersey* and traveled westward. After a short stop at Pearl Harbor they zigzagged across the ocean to Eniwetok, arriving on February 1, 1945. Soon after his arrival he ran into another UVM friend of ours, Allen "Red" White. Larry and Red were basketball teammates in college. He informed Larry that Misty Rice, my college roommate, had just left in the convoy headed toward Iwo Jima with the 5th Division, Charlie Company, 28th Marine Regiment.

On February 2, 1945, Larry arrived at Guam. While on Guam Larry ran into Billy "Ox-Bow" Muir, his friend from Dartmouth and Burlington. At that point many of the Marines on Guam were being shipped to Okinawa for replacements. Billy's orders soon sent him in the next contingent to Okinawa. In Larry's words, "The Ox-Bow left. As I said so long, the only visible identification was the familiar big grin beneath his steel helmet as he trudged off under the full complement of combat gear." This was the last he would see of Ox-Bow.

While on Saipan their platoon was involved in "extracting" the Japanese soldiers out the caves using small firearms and phosphorous grenades.

Sometime later as casualties came back from Okinawa for hospitalization, Larry found out from a friend, Eddie Sakovitz, that Billy Muir had been killed – shot through the head. Eddie, who was badly wounded, also told him that he saw Joe Margolis (UVM classmate and catcher on our baseball team) get killed. He was five yards away.

In June 1945 Larry's unit moved to Saipan with the 5th MP Battalion whose assignment was to rid the island of the remnants of the Japanese Army. In May of 1946 Larry returned to the states and was discharged. In 1950 he was called back in the Korean conflict. He joined the 2nd Division and was assigned to the 6th Marine Regiment. They were sent to Little Creek, Virginia and the Korean war soon ended.

When I moved to Burlington, Vermont, in 1950 I met Billy Muir's widow Marge. Sometime after when I was dating Mae Johnson, my future bride, I got Marge a blind date with an old friend of mine, Dick McKenzie, who I knew in Detroit. They hit it off beautifully and Dick and Marge were married. Soon after they moved to California, then Hawaii, and back to California. We visited them several times and were pleased to meet their lovely daughter Heather. Dick died several years ago and we continue to correspond with Marge and Heather.

Larry and I have been in close touch and we get together occasionally when we winter in Florida. Several years ago he wrote his memoirs of World War II, *Boots, Troops, and Hoops.* I gathered some of the information about Billy Muir from this. I will always cherish my friendship with Larry.

Harold Mayforth, Jr. – *Barre, Vermont*

Hal Mayforth was in the class of 1944 at the University of Vermont when I first met him. I was in the class of '43 and working as a scrub manager of football. He was a member of the Phi Delta Theta fraternity where I had several friends. In subsequent years and as a member of the varsity football squad I got to know Hal when I was manager. My most vivid memories of him were his performance as a speedy and gutsy halfback.

After the tragic days of Pearl Harbor I recall he was one of the first ones to volunteer and be inducted at Fort Devens, Massachusetts. During those years we all went our own ways as I was in the Navy and many of my other friends had volunteered and were serving all over the world.

I had no more contact with Hal until 1950 when I returned to Burlington, Vermont. He was in the automobile business with another close friend of mine, Torrey Carpenter. They operated the Saab car agency. Hal had returned from the war in September 1945 and continued his education at the University of Vermont.

I recently contacted him regarding his World War II experiences and he furnished me with some very interesting and exciting stories. Following are Hal's actual accounts of the history of his participation with the 4th Armored Division.

If I remember correctly the infamous day of Pearl Harbor occurred on a Sunday. Hence, it wasn't until the following night that a band of my fraternity brothers repaired to the bowels of the Hotel Vermont to usher in at our favorite waterhole, the Sugar House, the turning point of our youth. At midnight, the cut-off point, when we were full of beer and free popcorn, we thought it appropriate to sing the national anthem. We struggled through the first two stanzas without a hitch, but from there on the words escaped us. It was a combination of our physical condition and that patriotism had not made its full impact on us.

Shortly thereafter I concluded that I should enlist, but I wanted to be home for Christmas and New Year's. Therefore, I waited until February 17. Having ridden Army mounts at Fort Ethan Allen during the summer months of my Civilian Military Training days and since the horse had suddenly been deemed obsolete, I chose cavalry reconnaissance, mechanized.

I was inducted at Fort Devens, Massachusetts, then shipped to Pine Camp, now Camp Drum, New York, where I joined the 4th Armored Division. This was the outfit with which I would receive about 2? years of training and 8? months of combat.

My outfit landed at Utah Beach in France on D plus 38. There was then, for the first time, sufficient space to accommodate an Armored Division's men and vehicles. Hedgerow fighting was still in progress, and having parked our vehicles as the 25th Cavalry Reconnaissance Squadron, we were dismounted and had our first baptism of fire in that venue.

From the very outset I considered combat like a game of football with the opposition playing dirty. As the fighting progressed, I relaxed just having the gut feeling that I was invulnerable. My lot was to be a survivor.

An armored division was divided into three combat commands: A, B, and Reserve. Each combat command consisted of a reconnaissance troop, a tank battalion, an armored infantry battalion, and an armored field artillery battalion. When on the march with contact with the enemy having been lost, one of the three platoons of the reconnaissance were the lead element of the combat command. The three platoons of the reconnaissance troop rotated so that every third day a given platoon rode point.

Once we engaged the enemy we radioed back its strengths, disposition, and armor whereupon the tanks and infantry moved, throughout holding position. This having been affected we then moved out to protect our flanks.

I came through the Battle of the Bulge unscathed. The 4th Armored, Combat Command "B" was the first unit into Bastogne. Our fearless leader was a 28-year-old West Point graduate, Colonel Creighton E. Adams, later to become CO of all operations in Vietnam.

While we were in training my rank was that of a corporal–my duties, that of the troop's motor pool clerk. My duties involved keeping maintenance records of our 40 vehicles. I was also watchdog of all our equipment. This meant that when the troops went on bivouac or maneuvers I remained behind. To my mind, this duty was created in heaven, and I had no reason to forsake it. About four months previous to our commitment to combat, however, this prize position was eliminated, and I was assigned as Scout Corporal in the 3rd Platoon.

In combat, through attrition, I gradually climbed the ladder of command from Scout Sergeant to Platoon Sergeant. In spite of an increase in responsibility I was unable to shake my position in lead vehicles. The Scout Sergeant rode in a jeep, the point vehicle, the Scout Corporal in the second jeep. The Platoon Sergeant rode in an M8 armored car behind the first two jeeps.

Early in December '44 our platoon leader, a first lieutenant, was evacuated because of wounds and I took over as acting platoon leader.

On February 28, 1945, my habit of leading a charmed existence came to a mild end when approaching a small German farm community we knew in advance was defended. I was dismounted with my Scout Sergeant during the ensuing firefight when small arms fire hit the inside of my right ankle. It completely demolished my boot, drew blood, but required nothing but a sprinkling of sulfur powder and a bandage. It was a cheap Purple Heart.

The following day, I was designated to lead a patrol to determine if there was any enemy activity in a wooded area on a hill about a mile to our left flank. When we arrived there we found evidence of them having just evacuated that position. Then as we traversed an open field to further investigate some woods below, all hell broke loose. We received heavy small arms fire from Germans obscured by the vegetation. I yelled for the patrol to retreat, but while I lingered to return fire, I was hit in the right forearm and the right thigh. Fortunately, I was ambulatory, but by the time I reached our lines, I had lost so much blood that I was woozy.

For me the war ended right there. I was certainly impressed by the efficiency and speed with which I was rushed to a field hospital, to a base hospital, then flown back to a permanent installation in Bristol, England. My arm was operated on in Bristol, but because scar tissue had adhered to the ulnar nerve, further surgery was forthcoming at the Newton D. Baker General Hospital in Martinsburg, West Virginia.

Following is an excerpt from a selection "Cowboys and Germans," by John J. DiBattista, 4th Armored Division, 25th Cavalry Reconnaissance Squadron, "B" Troop, 3rd Platoon, in the book, *The Long Road*. It is in reference to a scouting assignment by Lieutenant Wiley to DiBattista.

So Wiley's talking to us: Who can handle a. 30-caliber machine gun?

At least I knew what that weapon was. I knew it blindfolded. I raised my hand.

He said to me, "Okay, you go with Sergeant Mayforth."

Mayforth was the scout sergeant. He was incredible. Without his glasses, he was as blind as a bat. He was also the bravest man I ever met. A little reckless at times. His father was a colonel in the despised Air Corps, and that was held against him. He was a maintenance clerk in the motor pool, then when a jeep unit was lost they made him a Scout Sgt. None of those corporals who were scout corporals came running. It was automatic promotion, but nobody wanted that job. I was assigned as his machine gunner and radio operator. What did Patton always say, "L'audace, l'audace, tujours l'audace." (*Audacity always*). Mayforth had that personified. He was daring. He was cultured. Spoke a smattering of French.

Just before the Battle of Arracourt, a big tank battle, when we were pinned down by mortar fire, Mayforth showed he was fascinated with explosives. There was a small mortar round, a dud. The fins were sticking up out of the ground. Mayforth goes over to it. Here's a highly intelligent guy who's so inquisitive about this thing! We're all standing around saying, "Don't touch it!"

"It takes nerves of steel!" he said. And he touched the thing! We talked him out of picking it up. Maybe he was just pulling our chain.

After Hal was wounded and returned to the States, he was on a sick furlough and spent some time working at the Nash Kelvinator Company in Dayton, Ohio. He was discharged on September 17,1945, and returned home to Burlington, Vermont, completing his education at the University of Vermont. He married a Brattleboro, Vermont girl, Catherine White. They had three children: Hal III, Marcy, and Peter. Peter is at the ski resort at Mammoth Lakes, California. Marcy is a very talented potter and shows her excellent work at many of the craft shows. Hal III is an artist and cartoonist whose work has appeared in *Newsweek, US News and World Report, Forbes, AARP,* and many other magazines. In 1993 he was the winner as the "Best" in magazine and book illustration, by the National Cartoonists Society. He graciously contributed the accompanying illustration relating to his dad's World War II exploits.

Graduation

It was a cold January day, about 15 degrees below zero. It was 1943 and we were graduating from the University of Vermont. My mother and father had driven 400 miles from North Tonawanda, New York, to attend my

Dad and Mom

graduation from college. That evening we graduated 44 students. There were 38 men and six women. Twenty eight were engineers, and I was one of the mechanical engineers. The marshal for the candidates was a close friend of mine, Eddie O'Connell. Jim Tennien, another close friend of mine, received the Edmund Little Cup for excellence in mechanical arts and was an honor graduate in the Reserve Officers Training Corp. Another friend, Howard C. Vreeland from Rutherford, New Jersey, also received a degree.

That evening was the end of my college experience. My class had started as freshmen with about 50 candidates. The dean of engineering had welcomed us and said that of all the 50 freshmen about 25 of us would graduate. He was almost right. For whatever reasons 22 didn't make it.

Some statistics of note on that graduation day,1943:

On the stock market there were 771,275 shares traded and 875 issues were transacted. Lockheed was at 18, Packard at 3 and General Motors at 45. Joe Dimaggio and Dorothy Arnold were reconciled, Joe quit baseball and joined the armed forces. Hank Mazur, the U.S. Army football captain graduated from West Point. Thirty-six hundred new cars were rationed for January. The book *Guadalcanal Diary* was on sale for $2. Canada Dry was 15¢ for the large bottle. Toothbrushes were 14¢ and men's trench coats $3.96. Anacin Tablets were 29¢ and dry cleaning was 50¢. Wax beans were 19¢ lb., roast beef 25¢ lb., rib roast 27¢ lb. and frankfurters 25¢. The local movie theater was packing them in to see Jimmy Cagney in *Yankee Doodle Dandy* for a whole quarter.

Signin' Up

The rest of 1942 and into 1943 we were all concerned about the war and it was not uncommon to see some of our classmates leave college and go into the service. We all knew that as soon as we graduated we would be putting on some kind of a uniform.

After graduation I went home and decided to volunteer for the Navy. As a graduate mechanical engineer I applied for a commission.

My brother Jim, who had graduated in 1941, was working in Rochester, New York, for the Bausch and Lomb Optical Company. They were working on top-secret bombsights and other critical defense projects. When I graduated Jim decided to volunteer for the Navy with me. We both proceeded with our applications and had our physicals scheduled in Rochester. We reported to the Navy office and were assigned physicals by Dr. Jim Jordan. In our first visit with Dr. Jordan he tested our eyesight and my brother found out that he was colorblind. He had been hoping to get in the Naval Air Corps but now found out that this was disqualifying. He could, however, continue to apply for an engineering specialty in the Navy.

During my physical I was mostly concerned with passing the weight requirement. I was about 5'7" and weighed somewhere around 120 pounds. Dr. Jordan informed me that 125 pounds was the minimum for my height and to report again to complete the physical in two days. He suggested that a diet of bananas and plenty of water might help me meet the minimum. After two days on a diet of bananas and water Jim and I reported for our final physicals. Needless to say I felt more like a chimpanzee than a Navy recruit. In any case the diet proved to be a success, as I tipped the scales at 126 lbs. I still think that Doc Jordan had his thumb on the scales.

After our physicals and our applications had been completed, Jim and I went back home and waited for the Navy decision. When I received my orders and my commission as an Ensign, I was assigned to an indoctrination school at Fort Schuyler, New York. Jim received his commission as an Ensign as an engineering specialist in the Navy Air Corps. We were now ready for our careers in the Navy.

Navy Training School of Indoctrination

Fort Schuyler in the Bronx, New York City and Boston Navy Yard

On March 29th, 1943, I donned my Ensign's uniform and boarded the train for New York City. At the age of 21 I was ready to embark on my career in the U.S. Navy. Arriving at Fort Schuyler I joined a class of 32 other new U.S. Navy officers. Most of these men were college graduates with engineering degrees, plus a few lawyers and miscellaneous other career people who received commissions. Fort Schuyler was to be the site of our indoctrination into the Navy. We had a considerable amount of classwork including the study of Navy rules and regulations, the blue jackets manual, and two or three other Navy courses to instruct us in the basic principles of Navy life. We also had considerable exposure to marching and close order drill. Most of us had had a couple of years at college in Reserve Officers Training Corps, which was mandated in all Land Grant Colleges. During my freshman and sophomore years we had full courses taught by United States Army officers. Military life was not a new experience for most of us.

The ages of most of the men were from above 21 to the middle 40s. Some of these men had been in specialties such as aspects of boating or marine law and had unique qualifications for many Navy assignments. It was interesting for me to meet men from all over the country who were leaving civilian life for navy careers.

One sunny day when we had some spare time I decided to take off my shirt and stretch out in the sun for rest and maybe a golden tan. It so happened that my resting spot was in full view of the commanding officer's second story office. To my surprise an orderly came down and told me that the skipper would like to see me. I quickly donned the rest of my uniform and proceeded up to his office. He told me that in the Navy there were rules against being sunburned. This was classified as disorderly conduct and as serious as contracting a venereal disease ('cept a whole lot easier to take care of!). Needless to say I was pretty shook up at being reprimanded by the skipper. My sunbathing ended that day, especially in full view of the commandant's office.

During the periods of close order drill we were all tested. We all took turns giving orders and running regular drill periods with our men. One very hot day when it was my turn to drill the men I called them to order. I gave several orders of *present arms, parade rest* and on my last command I said, "*Company dismissed.*" Immediately everybody broke ranks and left the parade ground. Our instructor was non-plussed at my dismissal of the company. Dismissal on a hot day was a nice break for the rest of the guys and I was a real hero to cut short our drill period. I'm not sure our instructors were thrilled, however.

Fort Schuyler Navy Training School of Indoctrination Graduation Class

Our indoctrination school ended on May 21, 1943. My next orders detached me from instruction at the Naval Training School and directed me to proceed to Boston, Massachusetts. I was to report to the commandant of the first Naval District for temporary duty under instruction at the Boston Navy Yard. This was to be about a month's tour at the Navy Yard in Boston observing construction of new naval vessels and aspects of naval architecture.

After reporting for this duty I had to find living quarters in Boston for approximately a month. Checking with the Naval office I found out that Admiral Byrd's wife had several rooms in their Beacon Hill home and there was a vacancy for about a month. This was a great break for me and I gladly went over and talked to Mrs. Byrd. She was extremely nice to all Navy officers and gave me a room. Living in Admiral Byrd's home was a great treat. We were allowed and encouraged to use his study and office and read many of his books. He had a marvelous collection of memorabilia from his great Antarctica expeditions. As I recall there were several polar bear rugs scattered about his office. Admiral Byrd at this time was on duty in the Pacific Theater. We unfortunately never got to meet him personally but it was a great thrill to live in his home. Another room was rented to a young man from Switzerland named Conrad Hurliman. Conrad was employed with the Maggi Company and had been sent to America to learn American business methods. He was a great guy and I enjoyed his company. We spent several weekends in Gloucester where some friends of his had a summer home.

Each day at the yard was spent in various phases of ship building and observing ship construction from the drawing board to the day of christening. It was especially interesting to see so many "Rosie the Riveters" working on naval vessels that would soon be participating in the war.

One of the highlights of this tour was a Navy flight on a practice bombing and dive-bombing of some targets off the coast of Boston. Flying in one of these Grumman fighters was a real thrill for a guy who had never flown in a plane.

Further directions in my orders were to proceed and report to the commandant First Naval District for temporary duty under instruction at the Navy Training School for Salvage, New York City.

United States Navy Training School

Pier 88, New York, New York

On July 2, 1943, my further orders sent me to the United States Navy Training School for Salvage at Pier 88 on the Hudson River. This pier was the site at which the French liner *Normandie* was berthed. On February 9, 1942, this majestic ship, that was being converted to a troop carrier, caught fire. The fire started when a civilian worker was using a blowtorch in the Grand Salon and sparks ignited the burlap wrappings on some stacks of life preservers. It spread rapidly and soon was burning out of control. Tugs and fireboats poured water on to the superstructure of the *Normandie*. The ship became top-heavy, listed to port, rolled over, and lay on its side in about thirty feet of water.

The Normandie in 1936.

The Normandie rolled over in 1942 after the fire.

The men in our group who reported with me on that July day were as follows; Ensign **Francis I. Babcock**, Ensign **John E. Davis Jr.**, Ensign **Jesse V. Fardella**, and Ensign **Ralph L. Fischer**.

The first thing we did was to go through the physical examination. It was the usual examination, but the major part of it was to go through the decompression chamber to determine whether we could withstand the pressures associated with diving. A decompression chamber is a large cylindrical unit with several benches for the subjects undergoing the test. The procedure was to increase the pressure to the equivalent of somewhere around 150 feet of water. As the pressure increased it was necessary for us to continuously 'pop' our ears to equalize the pressure on our eardrums. As it proceeded to increase we noted that our voices reached a greater pitch and we began sounding like Mickey Mouse. Our conversations became funnier and funnier as our voices kept changing. Finally we approached the maximum depth that was required and they began to decrease the pressure, comparable to ascending from a dive. It was necessary to decompress at various intervals in order to eliminate the possibilities of getting the bends – caused by the bubbles of nitrogen released into the bloodstream and lymphatic fluids by decreasing pressure. This happens as pressure increases and nitrogen begins to enter the bloodstream. It was necessary to stop for about 15 minutes at each interval. Finally we reached atmospheric pressure and the test ended. All of us passed this test without any problems and we were ready to proceed for our first dive.

That night we reported to our assigned diving instructor who that night was **Willie Harmon**. Lt. Harmon was one of the men who had participated in the rescue of the crew on the submarine *Squalus* that sunk while on a test dive on May 23, 1939.

The USS *Squalus*

The story of the *Squalus* was told in the book *The Terrible Hours,* by Peter Maas. Excerpts from this remarkable rescue are used here.

On Tuesday May 23, 1939, the newest submarine of the American fleet was the USS *Squalus*. The submarine was 210 ft. long, 27 ft. wide, an attack speed of 16 knots and an underwater speed of 9 knots.

Her commander on May 27th, 1939, was Lieutenant **Oliver Naquin,** who had 55 men under his command. As with any new submarine, a series of test dives are done to prove the watertight status and working conditions of all systems on the boat. This particular test dive was to be at a depth of 250 ft.

At 8:30 A.M. Lt. Naquin gave the order to rig for diving and received the all clear signal. With the control board reading all systems green, the men in the control room were completely surprised when they heard, over the battle phone, screams that the engine rooms were flooding. With the rear engine and torpedo rooms flooding, the weight became too much for the ballast to compensate and she began a plunge at a 50 degree angle to the bottom. Touching down stern first, the surviving crew members were lucky that although she was 243 feet deep she had settled evenly on her keel.

One of the modern amenities of the ship was a buoy that held a telephone and attached to the sub by a communications line. For hours the remaining crew would hang their hopes upon this buoy. Each one of the crew was aware that the general belief was, if a submarine went down, it was as good as lost. In the entire history of the submarine, no rescue attempts over 200 feet had been successful. At 243 ft. it would be virtually impossible.

Thankfully for the crew, former submarine commander **Charles Momsen** had designed and built a rescue chamber that had yet to be tested during an actual emergency. The chamber was comparable to an oversized tumbler that had been turned upside down – a tumbler that would have to make four trips down to the submarine before all 33 men could be brought up. During each trip two divers would have to go down with the rescue chamber, seal it to the escape hatch of the sub, and then transfer nine men into it for the long trip to the surface. The first three trips went without a hitch but after some broken cables and a series of other problems the fourth one seemed plagued from the start. Eventually this last trip was completed with the last man out of the rescue chamber, and the last man to leave the *Squalus*, her skipper Lt. Oliver Naquin. According to naval logs, he would make this step one minute before the 39th hour since the time he had given the order to dive.

Months later, the *Squalus* would be salvaged, refitted, and reconditioned on May 15, 1940 as the newly named *Sailfish*. She would serve bravely and honorably during the remaining years of World War II.

Three of these heroic men were to receive the Congressional Medal of Honor for their extraordinary heroism in saving the crew of the *Squalus*. Our diving instructors at Pier 88 included these men: **John Mihalowski**, **Orson Crandall**, **James McDonald**. **Willie Harmon** received the Navy Cross.

First Dive

We were on the night crew for our first diving instructions. The first thing that our instructor did was to introduce us to the equipment or diving suit. He proceeded to show us a diving helmet and indicated the various controls inside and outside of the helmet. There was the chin valve with which you could expel all the air out of the suit or, with the aid of the air control valve, add air to the suit. They then proceeded to show us how to get into the diving suit, put on the diving shoes and the weighted belt, place the helmet on the breastplate, and complete the

My graduation picture from Diving School at Pier 88

preparation for the dive. Each helmet contained a telephone for continuous communication with the surface unit and the diving attendant who had constant contact with the diver.

After all these instructions Harmon said, "OK guys, who's first?"

Needless to say there wasn't a rush to be the number one victim. We all took our turns and I guess I was about number four. At that time I weighed about 126 lbs. and the complete diving suit weighed about 190. I sat on the diver's stool and the crew proceeded to dress me. The tender then guided me over to the diving ladder and I descended the ladder into the very black looking water of the Hudson River.

I stepped down each rung of the ladder, grabbed the descending line and slowly went down to the bottom of the river in about 30 feet of water. The bottom of the Hudson River is not a lovely sandy bottom like the Caribbean. I sunk down into about three or four feet of silt and mud. I notified the diving platform and my tender that I had successfully reached bottom and was instructed to sit there for a few minutes and try out the various controls such as the chin valve and air control valve. During all this it was necessary to continuously pop my ears as I descended to the bottom to equalize the pressure and not burst my eardrums.

As I sat on the bottom of the Hudson River silt, with no visibility, in cold water and a reasonable amount of apprehension, I wondered, "What the hell am I doing down here?"

I had dreamed of joining the Navy and being assigned to some exciting duty on a destroyer or a battleship and sail off on the high seas to do battle with the enemy fleet. But here I was trapped on the bottom, in a diving suit, in the dirtiest water I had ever seen. This is what I was told to do and so I was determined to go ahead and be a salvage diving officer. Some guys did leave because of claustrophobia or other physical problems but all the guys in our group stuck it out.

When we arrived at Pier 88 we were informed that there was no housing availability and we would have to secure an apartment while we were training. We were fortunate enough to find a very nice apartment at Mitchell Place on the East Side of New York City. Three of us – Jess Fardella, Bob Gerwig – and I, subleased an apartment from a radio executive for our stay in New York.

Each morning we would get up at about 0700 and take the crosstown bus to Pier 88 for diving school. The diving training consisted of classroom courses in navy architecture, salvage procedures, and other training relating to Navy salvage. There were day and night shifts as the diving school ran around the clock. It didn't matter whether we were diving during the day or night because the water was so dirty we couldn't see anyway.

There was a whole series of exercises in which we were instructed to take down a bag full of pipe fittings and reassemble them on the muddy bottom of the Hudson River. One of the more difficult exercises was to take down a piece of wood about the size of a railroad tie to the bottom of the river and then proceed along the bottom to a designated point, and release the wooden tie. It's obvious that if you couldn't hold on to the timber during this procedure it would float to the top before you finished taking it to the required point along the muddy bottom.

Another one of the tests was to take about 10 pieces of wood down to a stage and build a box with a hammer and nails. To keep the wood pieces from floating to the surface it was necessary to place them under the staged table so they wouldn't float to the top. It was not uncommon for the pieces to break loose from your grasp and pop up to the surface. Generally because of the telephone in each diver's helmet we could hear the expletives when he would lose a piece of the wood. As I recall when I went through this particular exercise I brought my finished box to the surface and Willie Harmon with a flowery expletive said it "looked just like a f____ing chicken coop" instead of a box.

As you can imagine the Hudson River in New York in those days was not necessarily as clean as it is now. Among the flotsam and jetsam were various forms of trash including a plethora of used condoms. We called them "candy bar wrappers " and it was not uncommon to come up from a dive with several of these on your diving helmet and breastplate. We ran a little contest to find who could have the most wrappers on his helmet after any dive. I believe the record stood at about nine. Needless to say it was somewhat embarrassing as visiting relatives observing some of our diving procedures would see some of the objects encountered during a dive.

Many of the routine tests that we had to perform included procedures for patching and repairing damaged ships. We learned to use acetylene cutting torches and welding equipment adapted to underwater uses. It was amazing how it became possible to do all this work underwater, wearing such heavy and bulky equipment. Nevertheless, the Navy salvage school did prepare us for a variety of challenges. The motto was "a Navy salvage diver can do anything," and it became quickly apparent we were being trained to fulfill this challenge.

Much of the diving work on the sunken *Normandie* was done by many of our enlisted personnel who were being trained at the school. The guys that were diving on the *Normandie* quite often had souvenirs from this beautiful ship, such as some of the porcelain tableware complete with monogrammed silver utensils.

While the training was pretty difficult and arduous work, there were some pluses at having the opportunity to live in New York during this period. The civilian population was extremely kind and went out of their way to keep the soldiers, sailors, and marines happy. Mitchell Place where we lived was an area of some degree of affluence. We were often invited to the beautiful apartments of some very kind New Yorkers. One night we were invited to dinner by Nancy Wicker, whose mother was the "Singing Lady of Radio" at that time. We played a game of Charades with the "Easy Aces" of radio fame and other radio personalities of that era.

One of the highlights of living on Mitchell Place was that Madeleine Carroll, the beautiful movie actress, had a place in the same building. We used to hang around the lobby so that when Madeleine got on the elevator we would have the privilege of riding with this lovely lady.

Our Deep Dive

We would dive off the platforms adjacent to Pier 88 during the routine tests and tasks that we had to do. One of the basic requirements before being certified was that each diver had to go on a deep dive. The deepest spot in the Hudson River that time was beneath the George Washington Bridge. The depth of the river there was approximately 100 feet.

The normal procedure was to take about six of our divers with the diving instructors and proceed to the area around the George Washington Bridge. Here we would anchor the diving barge and set out a descending line to the bottom of the river. The purpose of the deep dive was to expose us to a longer time under a greater pressure than the 30 feet we had been diving in. Regular air is actually a gas mixture consisting of 80 percent nitrogen and 20 percent oxygen. For a diver the culprit in this combination is the nitrogen.

If he comes up too rapidly after a descent he will be stricken by the bends. The name comes from the tortured shapes into which it can twist its victims. When a man is subjected to great pressure, not all the nitrogen he breathes in his air supply can be exhaled. Some of it instead, is carried by the blood into his body tissues in much the same manner that carbon dioxide is forced into carbonated drinks. As long as the pressure is decreased slowly, the nitrogen exits as innocently as it entered. But if the pressure is lowered too fast, it forms a froth of bubbles like a bottle of ginger ale that has suddenly been uncapped. These bubbles tend to concentrate at the bone joints. The pain even in a mild attack is excruciating. In a severe case the bubbles clog the veins completely and can cause instant death from a heart embolism.

Still more insidious during a deep dive is the way nitrogen attacks the central nervous system and drastically affects the muscular coordination. Eventually, along with a carbon dioxide buildup inside the helmet, it renders the diver unconscious.

Knowing all this, it was imperative that we all go through the experience of a deep dive. We would take turns slowly descending the line to the bottom of the Hudson River. We were constantly in touch with the diving tender who was holding our airline. After perhaps a half-hour on the bottom of the river we were instructed to slowly proceed up the descending line to various intervals for decompression. These periods of decompression would allow all the nitrogen out of our body tissues back into the breathing air. There were probably about 4 or 5 different levels at which we would stop while ascending to the surface.

In preparation for our deep dive we were told to get a good night's rest and abstain from any alcoholic beverages or caffeine. Needless to say we were all somewhat apprehensive and carried out these orders explicitly. However, one of the guys who was a little more concerned than most of us, thought that a few beers might relax him. We were not aware of this until he was going down the descending line to the bottom of the river. He will remain nameless but it was obvious that "Charlie" was slightly inebriated. When he got all the way down he began laughing and singing as he sat on the bottom of the river. All was well until we ordered him to begin his ascent up the descending line. He started laughing and said he liked it down there. All we could do under the circumstances was pull him up through the various levels of decompression. After a lot of hauling and grunting we got Charlie aboard. For the deep dive he received a passing mark, and we all had a lot of laughs.

Demolition of the USS *Chilore*

Little Creek, Virginia

Diving at the site of the USS *Chilore*

For further training and experience with demolition underwater, we were sent to Little Creek, Virginia, to dive on the sunken USS *Chilore*. This boat had sunk off the coast of Virginia during the past year and was to be the scene of our training for underwater demolition. There were about ten ensigns in our group and this project was under the direction of Commander Ankers who was a veteran of marine salvage in the Mediterranean.

We all reported for this assignment on December 6, 1943. We went aboard a small YP, which was to be the ship from which we operated. The first day aboard we were to become familiar with dynamite, primacord, and the equipment to facilitate blasting operations. That first morning our instructors put us to work preparing the sticks of dynamite and primacord, that we had to assemble as a large, long dynamite string to circle the sunken ship.

We went ahead and proceeded to handle the dynamite gingerly as we were not fully aware of its sensitivity. We also proceeded to do this work with our bare hands. Needless to say we did not realize that the nitroglycerin on our bare skin would create severe headaches. That first morning it was obvious that we should have worn gloves for excessive handling of dynamite. The old Navy veterans had a few laughs about us rookies getting headaches. This hazing was also part of our training.

After a couple days of preparing the strings of primacord and nitroglycerin we were ready to proceed to dive on the wreck and place the charges. The ship was sunk in about 30 or 40 feet of water and the purpose of clearing the wreck was so that other ships would not hit the sunken vessel. We all proceeded with inspection dives and then placed the dynamite strings around the ship to prepare for demolition. This took three or four days to fully encircle the wreck.

Late in the afternoon on the fourth day Commander Ankers announced that we were ready to set off the charges. In order for our YP to clear the area before the explosion, it had to move some distance away from the sunken ship. It was obvious that someone had to be in a smaller boat with the detonators and reel out the detonating wire in preparation for setting off the charges. Commander Ankers assigned Jesse Fardella and myself to get in a small boat and set off the blast.

Jess and I got into the boat. We were cast off with the reel of blasting wire to gradually pay out the wire and slowly drift away from the blasting area. By now it was pitch dark and all we had was a couple of flashlights and a pair of oars to slowly row away as I gradually let out the wire from the reel. It was kind of windy that night and became more difficult to know whether we were drifting away as I let the wire out. Finally we were running out of wire and presumably had drifted away from the wreck, so we figured with a little luck we were clear and could push the plunger on the blasting machine. Jess said, "OK Joe," and we both whispered a quiet prayer. I pushed the handle on the detonator. There was a short pause before a sudden huge explosion some distance away from our rowboat. We knew that we were safe. Our demolition of the *Chilore* had been a success and we were ready to climb back on the YP with our buddies. Soon we saw the lights of the boat approaching us and we were able to climb back aboard to be congratulated by our grateful buddies.

The next day, December 23, two days before Christmas, we took the train back to New York and Pier 88 for more diving training.

Salvaging the *Normandie*

During the time at Pier88 salvaging efforts on the *Normandie* continued with many Navy divers working on the overturned vessel. Much of the superstructure was cut off and efforts to compartmentalize sections of the ship were completed. Pumps were located on various sections of the upper side of the ship in preparation to pump out the water when the ship was considered watertight.

Before the fire, plans were to convert the *Normandie* to a troop transport to be renamed the USS *Lafayette* in honor of the brave French general who aided the American rebels during the revolution. Work had scarcely begun when the fire changed all those plans.

On August 4, 1943, pumping began and gradually the ship began to right itself. On August 9th it had approached a 45 degree angle, had buoyancy in the stern, and was prepared for the final righting process. On October 27, 1943 the once majestic ship was at long last on an even keel. The *Normandie* was righted but too late. She was no longer needed for the war effort. Declared surplus, she was sold and scrapped. The pride of France – swift, sleek, opulent – had sailed between 1935 and 1939 only. She was towed and pushed out into the North River and headed down toward the Statue of Liberty, that other magnificent gift of France.

On September 20, 1945, the big ship was declared surplus,

The Normandie righted again in 1943

The Normandie being cut up for scrap in 1947

sold to Lipsett, Inc., a New Jersey scrapping firm and ultimately sold for junk. On October 6, 1947, the last section in the boiler room was reduced to scrap. That evening the *Herald Tribune* editor looked at the final picture and scrawled the headline: "The End of a Proud Ocean Greyhound."

After we returned from Little Creek, Virginia, we were assigned to report everyday to the Staten Island Naval base at Thompkinsville. Each morning we would get up, take the crosstown bus to the subway, proceed to the Staten Island ferry, cross over to Staten Island and take another bus to the naval base. This was just more training to observe shipbuilding and improve our knowledge of navy ship construction.

During whatever spare time we had, Jess Fardella and I would visit Stillman's boxing gym and watch many of the boxers of that era doing their daily workouts. Jess was a big boxing fan as he had been an intercollegiate boxer at Penn State College. His senior year he was the Eastern Intercollegiate lightweight boxing champion. We watched boxers like Jake LaMotta, Rocky Graziano, Fritzie Zivic, and others prepare for their fights.

On some evenings if we weren't too tired we would go downtown to some of the jazz joints in Greenwich Village and listen to many of the great jazz musicians. Among those we heard were Pee Wee Russell, Georgie Brunos, Muggsy Spanier, Miff Mole, and Barret Deems. On other nights we might hit the 52nd Street music spots like the Hickory House and Kelly's Stables where Billy Holiday often sang.

At that time the musical *Oklahoma* was packing them in on Broadway. One night with a packed house they admitted about 30 servicemen for one dollar apiece for standing-room-only.

Overseas – *European Theater*

Casablanca, Morocco

We finally finished diving school in early March of 1944 and eagerly awaited our next assignments as full-fledged diving officers. Some of the guys were ordered to salvage vessels as senior salvage officers, others were shipped to the various fleets for assignment to Harbor Clearance Units and amphibious salvage.

Five of us were ordered to the Eighth Fleet in the Mediterranean area. Francis Babcock, John Davis, Jess Fardella, Ralph Fischer and I, were sent to Norfolk, Virginia, and reported to the USS *Card CVE 15* for transportation to the Moroccan Sea Frontier in Casablanca. This was our first real trip from United States to a foreign country. We were all excited at the prospect of finally going overseas to participate and do our parts as ordered. The trip was uneventful as we were able to avoid any submarines before we got to Casablanca.

The big thrill came on a Sunday morning when we caught sight of land and observed the beautiful white buildings in our first glimpse of North Africa. Casablanca was aptly named and this beautiful Moroccan city became our first landing in Africa.

We were eager to look around the city and saw many of the tourist sites. We got a look at the sultan's palace and even had a chance to go for a swim at the local beach. We were not alone on the beach as not too far away was a group of young Arab girls frolicking in the water. It soon became apparent that these girls were topless and we finally realized we were far from home. We were in North Africa and life was going to be different. I thought of the old song "How Ya Gonna Keep Em (Down On The Farm After They've Seen Paree?)"

On April 2nd we took a train from Casablanca to Algiers and from there to a small town called Dellys, that was the navy salvage base in North Africa. This was the local boat club and the site for further salvage assignments. After a couple days at this base we flew from Algiers to Palermo, Sicily, to join the harbor clearance unit. At that time there were some sunken vessels and beached Navy ships that the harbor clearance unit was working on.

Our group of officers was assigned to a villa for our lodging. These houses were obtained by the navy to house the members of our harbor clearance unit. Our particular villa was quite nice and different from many of our own homes. Jess and I shared a nice big double room. As we proceeded to look around the house, we noticed that the bathrooms had more than the usual number of fixtures. The additional fixture was a bidet, quite different from what we had in our own homes. Jess asked what this was for and I told him it was used to brush your teeth. The next morning Jess bent over to brush his teeth in the bidet. Turning on the water it squirted into his eyes and he soon found out that it was not for brushing his teeth.

Palermo, Sicily

During our diving operations in Palermo, Sicily, we operated in several groups on a variety of salvage projects. Jess and I would work on one of the diving barges in Palermo harbor while several of the other groups would work on specific ships that were either damaged or on the beach.

On one particular occasion, we had a Sicilian diver, who was familiar with the Palermo harbor and greatly aided us on several occasions. I recall his first name only – it was John. This guy was an excellent diver. On one occasion we were working with him in fairly deep water and he was down quite a long time. When we pulled him up from his dive he was experiencing extreme pain.

It was immediately obvious that John had a severe case of the bends. We quickly put his helmet back on and got him back into the water to the previous depth that he had been diving. As soon as we had increased the pressure his pains slowly subsided and we gradually decompressed him at several levels on his way back up. This was a rare exception as we were normally diving in only 30 feet of water. We were lucky to have Jess with us as he could speak fluent Italian.

One day we were assigned the duty of diving on the submarine nets stretched across the entrance of Palermo harbor. These nets were deep and functioned as a gate that would be closed every night to keep submarines from entering the harbor. Our assignment was to inspect the gates and make sure they were still functioning properly. Surprisingly enough, we found out that one of the whole bottom sections was not intact, and it soon became apparent that the harbor was not as secure as we thought it was. The next few days were spent in repairing the damaged submarine gates.

Quite often we did underwater demolition to destroy some of the sunken ships so that our vessels could dock safely. Underwater demolition is very dangerous and it was necessary to get our divers out of the water whenever we did any blasting. During air raids we were always instructed to bring all divers up.

Every time we set off underwater explosions there was a bunch of little Italian kids hanging around the docks. After each explosion these little guys would dive into the water and retrieve all the dead fish that were killed. They would carry an old sock in their teeth and stuff it with the dead fish. For many of them, it was the dinner that they would have that night. We also kept them supplied with plenty of chewing gum and candy.

My friend Jess's family had all come from Sicily and he knew the little town where his mother was born. One day we borrowed a command car and drove about 30 miles to Termini Imerese and went to the small church in that village. In his best Italian, Jess talked to the parish pastor and told him his mother's name and the approximate time of her birth. She never knew exactly on which day she was born and this was pretty important to her son. The old priest dug into the dusty old volumes of the church records. Amazingly he found out the exact day and the year in which Jess's mother was born. He then wrote out a new birth certificate and gave it to Jess.

We also asked him about some of Jess's other relatives, and he immediately told us where they lived and showed us how to get there. The old priest took us over, rapped on the door, and introduced one of their long-lost cousins from the United States. With lots of tears and kisses they were soon all over Jess and me. We had planned for this eventuality and were able to give them several big cans of coffee and a large box of groceries. This whole experience was very moving to us and after all the tears and laughter we climbed back in our vehicle and drove happily back to Palermo. It was a first-hand experience of how many of our ancestors remember and with great love welcomed their American *paisans.*

One morning in Palermo when we were working on one of the ships in the harbor we observed a Liberty ship leaving port and proceeding out toward the sea wall. We brought our divers up so that the ship's wake would not interfere with the dive. The big vessel was moving along at a fairly good clip as we stood on our diving barge and watched it. As we watched, it became apparent that the pilot was moving quite fast and should be turning very soon. He was headed straight for the seawall and was not changing course.

He didn't change course and the big Liberty ship under full steam crashed directly into the seawall. All hell broke loose and fire boats and other rescue equipment sped to the scene. Obviously the whole bow of the ship was severely damaged. The next day we found out that the skipper of the Liberty ship was DWI. You might expect that on some of our busy recreational lakes back then, but during the war in Palermo harbor it was quite a surprise. I don't know what happened to the skipper and I assume he must have lost his license.

Amphibious Salvage On LCI 40, Naples and Pozzuoli, Italy

On June 30, 1944, I received orders to report to the commander of Task Force Group 841 in Naples, Italy, for landing craft salvage duty on the *LCI 40.* I was detached from Palermo duty on July 3 and reported to the *LCI 40* on July 6.

LCI stands for landing craft infantry, the vessels are used to transport combat troops into the beaches during a landing operation. This was all in preparation for the landings in southern France on August 15, 1944.

Landing Craft Infantry boats were designed to deliver soldiers and marines quickly during an amphibious assault on enemy territory.

I had 20 years to go!

LCIs and their crews proved their worth during invasions in North Africa, Italy, D-Day, and in the Pacific. LCIs didn't share the limelight like the more glamorous aircraft carriers, battleships and destroyers. In fact they earned the name "Waterbug Navy," when an admiral looked down from his battleship and watched the LCIs down below scurrying back and forth, and commented that they looked like a bunch of waterbugs. The phrase stuck.

LCIs did not receive special names after fish, cities, states, famous people, or heroes, only numbers, therefore it was virtually optional for the skipper and his crew to name their LCI. Our ship was called "Life Begins at 40." One of the other unique names that one of the LCIs in our group had adopted was the *Bioya*. Upon closer inquiry to her skipper we found out that this meant "Blow It Out Your Ass" – a cute sobriquet if I must say.

The role of our LCI was to take troops into the beaches and stand by for any amphibious salvage that might be required. Each ship was assigned a salvage diving officer and about 6 salvage divers. These divers had specialties as carpenters, ship fitters, motor machinists, and boatswains. They were: **Harper** – Machinists Mate; **Brady** – Carpenters Mate; **Zemina** – Ship Fitter; **Hill** – Seaman; **Flowers** – Seaman; and **Daniels** – Seaman. Each ship had special pumps, anchors, diving and fire-fighting equipment.

When I reported I met our new skipper LTJG **Bernie Gigot**, the executive officer, Ens. **Don Stadfeld**, supply officer Ens. **Doc Grossman**, and Ens. **Paul Miller**. We were to become great friends during the next few months.

Most of the LCIs were berthed in the little town of Pozzuoli near Naples, Italy. This town is famous as the home of Sophia Loren who regrettably wasn't born until much later. It might have been more interesting duty if she had been around when we were there. Most of these ships had participated in the landings at Sicily, Salerno, and Anzio.

We were now getting ready for the southern France invasion.

Our diving and salvage crew on the LCI40: (clockwise) Hill, Brady, Daniels, Harper, Flowers, Corbett, Zemina

While we were in Pozzuoli we spent most of the time keeping the equipment in good shape for the coming operation. There wasn't much to do except try to keep busy during the day and maybe go ashore for few beers at night. On Sundays we could go ashore to the Italian churches and attend Mass. There was always a chaplain assigned to each group of ships and there were services to include all faiths.

One of my more interesting experiences was to go to confession to one of the local Italian priests. In order for them to hear our confessions the Catholic navy chaplain prepared a list of the most common sins that sailors were apt to commit. When you went to confession you pointed to the appropriate sin and also indicated the number of times it was committed. He would then point to a list that included the penance that you were assigned. It was a bizarre way to go to confession but it served the purpose. Generally the chaplains would have a general confession and absolution and we would all proceed to receive communion as usual.

On a ship as small as an LCI, that only had five officers, we had one steward's mate to attend the officers wardroom. Ours was a young guy named Sandy who took great care of managing the wardroom mess, Sandy and I became great friends. He was the only black sailor on the LCI. Sandy was a good ballplayer, so whenever we hit a port and had a few hours for recreation Sandy and I would toss the ball on the beach.

In World War II, most stewards mates were African-American. This clearly racial distinction for a particular job bothered me greatly and thankfully this racial delegating has changed in the modern navy.

An excellent movie, *Men of Honor*, has been recently produced depicting the true story of the first black salvage diver to be trained in the United States Navy. It is about Carl Brashear, born in 1931 to a sharecropper family in Sonora, Kentucky. He entered the Navy at age 17 in 1948. Immediately assigned to galley duties he observed the specialty of deep sea diving. Unheard of for a black sailor at that time, he applied for the Navy Diving School, Bayonne, New Jersey, and was admitted.

Overcoming adversity and resistance he became a Navy salvage diver. In 1966 he lost his left leg during the recovery of a nuclear warhead in the Mediterranean. Through his remarkable force of will Brashear convinced doubtful Navy officers that he was capable of performing in active duty, even as an amputee. He continued to dive and earned his master diver certification. In 1998 he became one of only seven enlisted men in history to be enshrined in naval archives with a 164-page volume transcribing an oral history of his life and career.

During the time we were in Naples we gave the crew as much liberty as possible. Because of the proximity of the ancient city of Pompeii, many of the sailors would go sightseeing and the Red Cross provided guided tours. Pompeii was the city that was completely destroyed when Mount Vesuvius erupted in the month of August 79 AD. The Tours of Pompeii were extremely interesting and gave us a glimpse of Roman life then. Archaeologists have uncovered a great deal of this city and much of it is remarkably intact. During these tours we were privileged to see the various areas of the city including the marketplace and many of the private homes.

One of the more interesting sections of the city was the red light district or Lupanari, where there were special rooms for the various services offered by the occupants. Above the entrance to each room was an artistic depiction of their particular specialty. During the tours the guides would often point out the fact that the symbol of fertility in Pompeii was a penis with two wings. It was not surprising that the enterprising guides were selling these tokens as souvenirs to the curious sailors. Much of the mail for the next few weeks to wives and girlfriends contained these interesting tokens of affection.

As the time approached for the southern France operation, all the ships had been briefed and we were preparing for the next big step.

Southern France Landings

In preparation for the landings in southern France our function as an LCI was to pick up army infantry in the Naples area and proceed to the rendezvous off the coast of Corsica near Ajaccio. After we had taken the army personnel aboard and before leaving Naples, the navy chaplain came aboard and said Mass on our ship. As was the custom at that time the Catholic chaplain gave a general absolution and communion to everyone.

We proceeded in our convoy and rendezvoused off the coast of Corsica. That evening General Montgomery came by most of the ships on a British cruiser and signaled "Good Luck" to us all. We all were quite anxious about the prospects of the landing and a quiet sense of concern prevailed. I remember vividly a practice followed by many of us, which was to take our wallets and enclose them in condoms to keep them dry.

Early the next morning as we approached the beaches the navy destroyers and cruisers began a terrific bombardment of the shore. The air corps preceded these salvos with heavy bombing of the coastal cities. We were to proceed to Red Beach and unload our

LCI Landing (Note German prisoners in center)

infantry. We were then to fulfill our role as a salvage vessel to aid any ships stranded on the beach or that might suffer damage. The major resistance consisted mostly of gun emplacements of 88s as there was no air cover at that time. One of these guns zeroed in on us but our skipper was able to skirt around a hill on the shore and evade the fire.

Most of that first day was spent pulling a few ships off the beach, and aiding others by taking their anchors out so they could retract. That evening, just before sunset, a single German plane, a Dornier bomber flew over at a very high altitude. All of our ships fired anti-aircraft guns but the plane was out of range. As we watched, the bomber dropped a glider bomb, that was controlled from the air-craft. This was a new type of weapon and glided down, slowly cir-cling, and zeroed in on one of our LSTs unloading on the beach. It hit dead on and exploded midships on the LST, starting a huge fire. This was the first radio-controlled glider bomb that we had seen. Needless to say it was an impressive yet sobering example of preci-sion bombing by the German air force. By this time, however, the German forces had withdrawn much of their strength from the southern France area.

Landing Beach Operations: San Raphael Vicinity

After the initial landings in southern France, our duties consisted mainly of aiding the various landing craft in the operations of unloading more supplies and additional army personnel.

During these operations we also worked with various British ships. Some of the British sailors became good friends of ours and we made exchanges of cigarettes for rum. It was a tradition in the British navy to give a daily ration of rum to each member of the crew. Ship's store on our LCI was selling cigarettes to the crew for about 50 cents a carton. Our Limey friends were having a tough time get-ting cigarettes, and needless to say rum was not very available in the U.S. Navy. So it was a good deal for us to swap a carton of cigarettes for about a pint of Nelson's blood as it was called. This was the real dark strong rum, so a pint of it produced considerably more pleasure than a carton of cigarettes, especially if you didn't smoke. Oddly enough, after a nice little buzz, it was not uncommon to experience a wicked headache the next day.

We got to know a group of Aussie soldiers and invited a half a dozen of them over to our ship for an early Thanksgiving dinner. We had a great time and felt obligated to share some of their Nelson's blood to go along with our Vermont turkey. Our cook had obliged everyone with all the fixings, and we had plenty of mashed potatoes, squash, cranberries, and hot gravy. As dinner proceeded and the food and rum dwindled, it came time for our guests from down under to get back to camp. After a few more choruses of "Good Night Lydies" and a few other ribald Australian sea chanteys, we loaded them into the captain's gig to go ashore. As there was some food left, we generously proceeded to put turkey legs, wings, mashed potatoes and gravy into their pockets for the next day. Our foreign relations with Australia had just reached an unprecedented high.

One day we received orders to tow a large section of Quonset pontoons from San Tropez to Gulf Juan. This was in a little village near Cannes, in southern France. This town was famous as a favorite place for Winston Churchill to visit and relax while painting the beautiful scenes of this lovely seaside village.

Our Navy had a PT boat base in this area and we were bringing more pontoons for their docks. Our divers were kept busy doing various underwater repairs to the various landing craft. We also supplied pumps, fire-fighting equipment, compressors and other services needed by all these vessels. One common problem was getting mooring lines tangled in ships propellers, which necessitated diving and sometimes acetylene torching wire lines.

We did give shore leave as often as possible and our sailors got a chance to taste some of the French wine. I believe there were quite possibly some other extracurricular activities.

On one of our visits to the beach, Paul Miller our supply officer and I had met several French girls in the Red Cross center. They were very nice and invited us to dinner at their home in the town of Draguignon the next day. We left the ship and got a jeep ride to their home. These girls were cousins and we met their parents, who were extremely kind to us. We had brought along some coffee and powdered milk as these things were very scarce at that time. They proceeded to produce a beautiful pork roast and we enjoyed a great dinner.

The highlight of the dinner was when their father took us down cellar and produced a lovely bottle of French wine they had hidden from the German occupation forces. These people were very gracious and grateful for the arrival of the American forces in their occupied land. After such a pleasant dinner we thanked our hosts and headed back to our ship. Fortunately, we were able to hitch a ride back on an army amphibious vehicle and the corporal in charge took us right back to our ship.

Back with the Harbor Clearance Group

Toulon, France

October 1, 1944, I was ordered to rejoin my old harbor clearance group, now working in the harbor in Toulon. I said my good-byes to all my good buddies on the *LCI 40*. It's always difficult to leave a bunch of guys you have lived so close to and gone through some terrific experiences with. In most cases this would be the last time I would see any of them. It was great to see the old Palermo group, however, and renew these friendships.

While I was on the *LCI 40* they had completed their work in Palermo and were assigned to proceed to Toulon, France. They had transferred all our equipment to the USS *Tackle* an older salvage ship, that had been converted from a lumber transporting ship to a salvage vessel early in the war. It had become known as the "Bucket of Rust" because of its age. This unit had sailed into the harbor at Port du Bouc and struck a mine as it was proceeding to the dock. Fortunately it was not severely damaged and all the salvage equipment was transferred to Toulon for use in clearing that harbor.

Toulon Harbor 1942

Scuttled French ships in Toulon Harbor being viewed by the Germans.

The harbor in Toulon was a real mess. The French Vichy fleet on November 27, 1942, as the Germans attempted to seize it, had been totally scuttled upon Admiral Darlan's orders, consisting of one battleship, two battle cruisers, four heavy and three light cruisers, 24 destroyers and 16 submarines. Thus the French battle fleet passed to neither side in the naval balance in the Mediterranean.

Before I arrived, the harbor clearance group had moved in to an old schoolhouse that had just been occupied by German officers. They obviously left in a hurry as much of their equipment was still there. One of the real prizes that they had left was a beautiful radio. It was called a Telefunken and fortunately had not been booby-trapped. There was also a fairly large group of prisoners. Many of them were Polish soldiers who had been forced into the German army. Needless to say these young men were happy to be captured by Americans and were employed in doing many odd jobs around our quarters. They were just young guys like us and were serving in the army as they were told to do. On one occasion we were reprimanded by some of our seniors for fraternizing with these men.

I'm sure some of ours who had been captured were not treated nearly as well by the Germans.

It was not long before the port of Toulon was sufficiently secure and our ships were able to use it effectively. The scuttled French fleet was still sitting on the bottom of the harbor as it was when we arrived.

We were soon ordered back to our salvage base in North Africa. We loaded everything on to the USS *Tackle* and sailed back to Dellys near Algiers. We were all looking forward to further assignment either in European or Pacific Theaters.

Arzew, North Africa

We arrived in Dellys, North Africa on December 4, 1944 and soon after were transferred to Arzew near Oran.

While we were waiting further orders I was assigned to be a demolition instructor to enlisted men. This work consisted of taking the men out into the desert and demonstrating various applications in the use of dynamite, TNT, and plastic C. I enjoyed working with explosives as we had utilized many of these procedures while clearing the harbors of Palermo and Toulon.

The Sermon on the (gun) mount

One Sunday in North Africa one of the fleet chaplains – I don't remember what this chaplain's name was but we'll call him Father Murphy, as that's a safe bet – came to Arzew to say Sunday Mass on the fantail of one of our ships. He completed the preliminary part of the mass and then climbed up on to a gun mount to give the homily of the day. His sermon dealt with many of the problems servicemen have away from home. He touched a lot on morality and the importance of marital fidelity and many of the other concerns with which most of us were confronted.

When he got to the subject of profanity and our various expressions during conversation he stated the following, "You know, boys, if they removed the word 'f___' from the English language, most of you would be speechless."

We all kind of knew this was true since this particular word was an integral part of our vocabulary. It was commonly used as an adverb, adjective, verb, and improper noun. I know now that in most modern-day movies, if this word were removed, they would be relegated to the archives of silent film.

I will always remember this sermon as this versatile word still can often be heard from some of my World War II golfing buddies.

During this time in Arzew and with the approach of Christmas, some of us decided to have a party for some of the French and Arab children in that area. My friend Jesse and I and some of the other sailors gathered a lot of candy, oranges, and some toys in the local area and prepared for the Christmas party. We selected a large room in one of the barracks, rigged up a Christmas tree and prepared for the party. I think there were about 50 little kids whom we had gathered together from the local town. When the time came to distribute the candy and gifts we attempted to pass the goodies out to the kids in an orderly fashion. Unfortunately these poor children hadn't been treated to a Christmas party for some time and practically knocked us over while we attempted to pass out the gifts. They had a wonderful time and it was great to see how excited these little people were to have somebody treat them to a party after seeing so much of war and deprivation.

That Christmas Eve there was a midnight Mass in the area and some of the Italian war prisoners had made up a choir and sang during the Mass. For all to come together and celebrate Mass so far from home it was a very impressive and moving experience.

On January 4, right after lunch, my roommate Wendell Alexander asked me to come into our room as he had something to tell me. I came and sat down wondering what was going on and soon found out. He had a telegram in his hand and said they had just received this from the Red Cross. He handed it to me and it read as follows; "Mother needed an operation, her heart failed her. She passed away December 27." The telegram was from my brother Mike. This was a great shock and surprise to me as I had just received a nice Christmas note from Mother and Dad a few days earlier.

I didn't remember the last time I had cried but it happened. I thanked Alex and took a walk to the beach and stared out into the Mediterranean for some time. I always feared that either Jim or I might not come back from the war and Mom would be a gold star mother. And now I was a gold star son.

Our skipper and all the rest of the guys were great to me during this time. Our commanding officer had immediately checked whether there would be an emergency leave for a death in the family. For security reasons there would be no leaves for anyone in the Mediterranean Theater. I had no way of knowing any of the details of Mother's death, but about a week later I received a long letter from my dad. The letter read as follows and was written in Dad's beautiful longhand script.

January 5th, 1945

My Dear Joe,

No doubt that by this time you have received the sad news about poor mother, it came as an awful shock to us all, but God knows best.

She had been suffering considerably and an operation was necessary. She had been going to a specialist in Buffalo for over six weeks having X-rays taken, blood tests, in fact a complete check out all over. Her gall bladder had to be removed at the recommendation of both the specialists Dr. Arron and Dr. Regan. They might have to give her blood transfusions, so they could go ahead with the operation. Her blood turned out to be fine. Up in every respect and no transfusion was necessary, so they operated on her Saturday December 23rd and everything looked fine. The operation was OK. They removed the gall bladder and she was coming along fine until Christmas morning when she had a bad spell out and got very weak. Tom, Mike, Loretta and I went over Christmas morning and they did a blood transfusion from Tom as Tom's and Mike's were the same as mother's, I believe 2A, Loretta and mine were the same 4A.

After the transfusion, she picked up and looked as if everything was going to be OK. She had another bad spell December 27th Wednesday so they called us over at 7:00 in the morning. She rallied again until 11:00 p.m. when she died. Dr. Regan was at the hospital at 10:00 and told Mike and I to go home as he figured she was coming along fine.

She had two glasses of orange juice and a cup of tea during the day and felt pretty good talking to us and knew everything that was going on. Michael went home about 10:00 to be with La La, Margaret and Marge. I told Tom we had better stick around which I am thankful to God we did, as we were with her to the last. May God have mercy on her poor soul.

The whole trouble Joe is that she worried too much all her life and that took so much out of her poor heart. It is awful lonesome without her, and must have been hard on you and Jim to be so far away.

Barbara came up from Rochester Friday the night before the funeral and she was buried Saturday December 30th. She had a beautiful solemn requiem High Mass. Father Malloy and Father Crotty where assistants to Father Hunt. She had many beautiful flower pieces and many Mass cards. Mike, Margaret, Mickey came up with us right after Thanksgiving, so Mother wouldn't be alone. They're still with us now and it isn't so lonesome with all of them around. Joe, mother is better off as she was a living Saint and all we can do now as Father Hunt said is to PRAY TO HER.

Barbara wrote you a letter, followed by La La and it took me till now to write. I came back to the shop today January 4th, I could not write at home. I don't know whether you can read this letter or not. Aunt Sarah called up from St. Petersburg Sunday, she had just gone home two weeks earlier as she was here since early September. Too bad she had gone. Aunt Rachel isn't so well now but Mike and Tom went over after her so she could see Mother before the funeral. Well Joe, I can't write any more for now as I want to write Jim. Received a letter you wrote December 24th today and I'm sure we will be hearing from you again soon. Will close for now. With fond love to you Joe,

From Dad

Marseille and Rome

A short time after Mother had passed away, our commanding officer, in order to give me a little vacation, issued me a new set of orders to proceed to Marseille, Naples, and Rome for conferences on salvage matters. This was primarily to give me an opportunity to see some of my old friends and visit Rome, which I had never seen.

On January 11, 1945, with orders to fly to Marseille I reported to the Algiers airport. Our transportation was to be on a U.S. Air Force transport plane that had several rows of bucket seats along each side. On boarding the plane one of my best friends from the USS *Tackle* was also going to Marseille. Lloyd Ewing, who had been the navigator on the salvage ship Tackle, joined me on the flight. We were also joined by one other passenger, a U.S. Army nurse. Lloyd Ewing had become a close friend by now and it was great to see him for this trip. He was kind of a relaxed character and not too fond of navy spit and polish. We both came aboard with small duffle bags apiece, but he had a large paper bag that he took special care of. Not too long after taking off Lloyd dug in to the paper bag and produced a couple of bottles of wine and some cold chicken. Not exactly in first class but the food was certainly comparable. We took off in a blinding rainstorm but that certainly didn't bother us. We arrived in Marseille in very high spirits.

I spent the next few days with some of my old salvage buddies working in the Marseille harbor. Several days later I climbed on a plane to Rome. The Red Cross had a tour of Rome that I was able to take. Part of the tour included a visit to St. Peter's and we hoped to have an opportunity to have an audience with Pope Pius the 11th. Fortunately we were able to do so and after a tour of St. Peter's we proceeded to the chapel for papal audiences. There were about 20 of us in all branches of the service and we went up to the altar and knelt in anticipation of the pope's arrival. He came out and spoke briefly to us in English and as he walked along we kissed his ring. As he extended his ring to me he asked me if I was an American sailor and I nodded yes as I kissed the papal ring. Naturally, this was a big thrill for me and a wonderful experience. I knew my mother was pleased.

On January 19, per my orders, I flew from Naples back to Oran and joined the rest of our group back in Arzew.

Back Stateside

On February 16, 1945, I received orders to report back to Pier 88 in New York for further assignment. The next day we were ordered to report to Oran for transportation to the States. Our transportation was the command ship USS *Catoctin AG C5*, which was returning to New York and had accommodations for several of us who were going back to the States.

On March 12 after an uneventful trip across the Atlantic we were finally seeing the beautiful Statue of Liberty, which represented everything that we were all fighting for. Coming into the harbor we were greeted by the welcome blasts of many tugboats as they knew our ship contained quite a few returning servicemen. As we tied up at the docks there were many booths with Red Cross personnel welcoming us home. There were all kinds of refreshments and oddly enough the beverage of preference was good old fresh American milk, which none of us had tasted since leaving home. I spent a few days in New York and then took the train to Buffalo. This was the first time I would see anyone since my mother passed away and I was very apprehensive.

When I arrived at the station my dad, my sister Loretta, and my Aunt Mamie were there to welcome me. There were lots of smiles and tears as we all hugged and kissed. It was great to be back home but the tremendous void that Mother left was tough to bear. I felt especially bad for my dad and my sister as we all had been so close for all our lives. I spent the rest of my leave visiting my brothers Tom and Mike and their families. Gas was rationed at that time but "Pop" Ramsey our city recreation director slipped me a bunch of gasoline stamps and I was able to bounce around town and see some friends. Most of my buddies were overseas but I did see many old friends.

After my brief leave I took the train back to New York and reported to Pier 88, the salvage base, for further assignment. The commandant informed me at that time that I was to be assigned to a new salvage vessel that was under construction in Texas. This was good news to me and the prospect of some stateside duty was welcome. At that time there was a salvage ship, which was a converted yacht, owned by the Vanderbilt family and given to the navy, operating in the New York vicinity.

I was temporarily assigned to this ship whose skipper was an old bosn's mate named "Bucky" Rogers. He was a great guy and was now a Lt. (jg) and Captain of the *Vagrant*. At that time they were raising a sunken ferry boat in Elizabethport, New Jersey, and training a new batch of salvage divers. This was great duty as we worked on salvaging the ferry and enjoyed being near New York City.

May 8, 1945: Germany formally surrendered. The war in Europe was over, but the war in the Pacific still raged. Because of that, it was premature to get too excited. We who were in uniform knew that the chances of of being killed through action were still all too present. Uncle Sam certainly was not declaring that our lives were our own yet, to do with as we would.

On June 3, 1945, my orders were suddenly changed and I was ordered to immediately fly to Pearl Harbor to report to the *ARS* 8, the *Preserver*, as senior salvage officer.

I flew by commercial airlines to San Francisco for further transportation to Pearl Harbor. I was fortunate to get a berth on the Pan-American clipper to Hawaii. At that time this was an overnight trip with sleeping berths on the clipper. Just as we were about to take off I was informed that an army major had pulled rank on me and would get my berth. So I sat up all night and we eventually flew into Honolulu.

At that time my brother Jim was in Hilo on the big island of Hawaii. Jim was with a naval air force Casu unit and had been overseas for about 18 months. I was excited at the prospect of seeing Jim after a couple of years. I had no way of notifying him I was coming to Pearl Harbor because of security reasons, so thought it would be a great surprise to him.

As soon as we landed in Honolulu I went to the Naval Air Station

My brother Jim Corbett and Harold "Misty' Rice in Hilo

and asked them to contact my brother in Hilo. They called the base and I asked to speak to Lt. James Corbett. After several minutes the sailor on the phone informed me that Lieutenant Corbett had, the day before, been sent back to the States on leave and further assignment. I immediately called the Port Authority at Pearl Harbor and was told that my brother was on a ship back to the States that left Honolulu that morning. My prospects of getting together with Jim had failed and I cried for the second time in the navy.

I then reported to the *Preserver* that was in dry dock being repaired. No ship ever has been more fittingly named than the USS *Preserver*. This repair and salvage ship of SerForPac had been hit by a Japanese bomb ... ripped by an 8-inch shell ... showered with shrapnel ... damaged by a near miss ... and all in all had 27 holes or dents in its hull and superstructure.

Yet not a single casualty had occurred aboard her. The bomb crashed into the motor room during the battle for Leyte Gulf – but didn't explode. The 8-inch shell dropped into the crew's washroom that was empty. A shell fragment slashed into an officer's bunk

but it was unoccupied. The closest call came when a motor machinist's mate was struck by a piece of shrapnel but it was the flat side of the fragment that hit him and he suffered no more than a bump.

I learned all this having read it in *All Hands* magazine when it was called the "Lucky P" This was to be my home for the next year and a half.

ARS8-USS *Preserver* – **Our home**

The *Preserver*

When I reported to the *Preserver* she was in dry dock at Pearl Harbor undergoing repairs from damages inflicted by Japanese bombers at Leyte Gulf on October 20, 1944. I was only aboard for a couple of weeks when repairs were completed, and we moved out of dry dock on the 29th of June. Lt. (jg) Charlie Richards was the acting

Captain C. B. Hiner and Exec. Officer and Navigator Lieut. Charles Richards

captain of the ship until the arrival of the new skipper, Lt. Commander C. B. Hiner who took command on July 6, 1945. Lt. Richards became the executive officer when Captain Hiner took over. Our new captain was in Navy parlance a "Mustang," which was the slang for a career Navy man who came up through the ranks and became a commissioned officer. These Mustangs were really the backbone of the U.S. Navy as they had many years of experience, working up through the ranks as enlisted men, and having sea duty all over the world.

Much of the information I will relate about the Preserver was gleaned from a handwritten ship's log sent to me by John Criscuolo of Brooklyn, New York, who was the chief yeoman on the ship since its commission on January 11, 1944.

At this time the officers aboard the *Preserver* were as follows:
Acting Captain and Navigator – Lt. **Charles Richards**, Reserve
Communications – Lt. (jg) **Robert Matthews**, Reserve
Sr. Salvage & First Lt. – Lt. (jg) **Joe Corbett**, Reserve
Asst. Salvage & Navigation – Lt. (jg) **Grant Harris,** Reserve
Gunnery – Ensign **Harold Timmerman**, Reserve
Chief Engineer – Chief Warrant **R. McCurry,** Mustang
Chief Bos'n – Chief Warrant **W. Brosey**, Mustang

When I reported I was assigned to be a roommate with Grant Harris whom I lived with until we were discharged. We hit it off very well and are great friends even until the present time. Grant was an excellent photographer and took many pictures of all the personnel on the ship and many of our experiences. He devised a photo enlarger and had his own developing darkroom. All these pictures during our *Preserver* tour were shot and developed by him.

Lt. (jg) Grant Harris – Salvage and Navigation, and Photographer

Grant was a forester, and living in Montana when he joined the navy. He was an ardent Mormon and the first one with whom I had been acquainted. I was a Roman Catholic and we had many philosophical discussions. I was greatly impressed by the devotion to his family and his faith, and I would certainly classify him as one of my finest friends. He had been recently married and most nights he would sit down and write a letter to his beloved Bea.

Lieutenant Joe Corbett – Senior Salvage Officer and First Lieutenant

While we were in Pearl Harbor, I found out that one of my closest friends, Don Kasprszak, who, I grew up with was with the marines and stationed at the marine base on the other side of the island. Don and I were from the same hometown of North Tonawanda and we had played baseball and basketball together. Don excelled in football and received a scholarship to Columbia University. He became one of the most outstanding quarterbacks in their history. He was able get a day off and we had a wonderful time getting together in Pearl Harbor. Don later became a surgeon and is still practicing medicine in Plattsburgh, New York, just across the lake from my adopted hometown of Burlington.

On June 20, 1945, our ship got out of dry dock and we began all our shakedown maneuvers in preparation for further duty. While we were in dry dock we were fitted with large extensions on each side of the hull to increase our stability and lower our center of gravity. Because of these larger additions to the hull it was necessary that we go through considerable testing and trial runs. It took almost a month for these maneuvers before we were in and out of dry dock once more and finally ready to sail.

Ensign Harold Timmerman – Gunnery Officer

On July 5, 1945, Lt. C. B. Hiner reported for duty and assumed command relieving Charlie Richards, who became the executive officer.

The second day after taking command Captain Hiner summoned me to his cabin, introduced himself, and started our conversation. His first remark was that he really didn't like the new young "90-day wonders" who had become officers in the Navy right out of college. Especially salvage officers, he said, as I guess he had had some previous negative experience with one of them. We had further conversation in which I discussed my earlier experience in the Mediterranean doing harbor clearance in the harbors of Palermo and Toulon and amphibious salvage on the *LCI 40* in the invasion and landings in Southern France. My duties aboard the *Preserver* were as senior salvage officer and first lieutenant. I was somewhat surprised and shocked at his attitude but was determined to do a good job under any circumstances. I thanked him for his frankness and left his cabin. So much for my introduction to our new skipper and the start of my duty aboard the "Lucky P."

After our new captain took command we continued all our trials and continuous testing of new equipment that had been added during our dry dock repairs. During all this work it was obvious that Captain Hiner,

Ensign Bob Matthews–Communications Officer

or "the Bull" as we affectionately called him, was an excellent ship handler as his many years in the regular Navy had prepared him well to maneuver a ship. There was considerable resentment as his attitude about "90 day wonders" soon became obvious, however, I was the first lieutenant during landing and anchoring operations. My duties at this time included the responsibility for all the deck crews in handling the lines or dropping anchor. It seemed about every time we came into a dock to tie up he would have some kind of an

Chief Warrant Officer R. McCurry – Chief Engineer

excuse to" eat my ass out" about any little thing that happened during these procedures. It became quite a joke when every time we tied up I would hear "Lt. Corbett report to the captain's cabin." I would report to his cabin and he would proceed to bitch about one little thing or the other that happened during these maneuvers. Our Chief Warrant Officer Brosey who actually ran the deck crew and was responsible to me for running the crew would just shrug his shoulders and laugh about the Bull's actions. Most of my fellow officers also experienced these continual rantings.

About a month and a half after Captain Hiner had taken command of the ship, he called me to his office. He informed me that he had just completed my current fitness report and that I should look it over. It is customary and even mandatory that if the commanding officer is considering an adverse fitness report he must show it to the subject officer before submission. I looked it over and it was obvious that I was getting relatively low marks on virtually every one of the rating factors. He had just been aboard the ship for a short time and was now making judgments about many things, that he obviously hadn't had time to observe. Naturally the whole procedure upset me greatly. I said that I didn't quite understand some of his observations, but if that's the way he felt I had no control over his judgment. There wasn't much more I could say so I excused myself and went back to my cabin.

Chief Warrant Officer W. Brosey – Chief Bosn

According to navy regulations if a superior gives you a fitness report that is derogatory you have the opportunity to write a letter expressing your opinion. I immediately sat down and proceeded to write my response to his action. I wrote a long letter describing my first interview with Captain Hiner in which he had stated that he disliked new reserve officers and especially salvage officers. I mentioned that he had a personal prejudice against me and cited all my previous experience and good record during my service in the Mediterranean. I signed the letter and gave it to the chief yeoman who brought it to the captain's cabin.

It wasn't much more than a couple of hours before I was called on the speaker advising me to come to the captain's cabin. I immediately reported to his cabin and when I arrived there the Executive Officer, Charlie Richards, was with him. The captain had my letter in his hand and also my fitness report. He handed my fitness report to Charlie and asked him to look it over. The exec took it and began

Our Salvage and Diving Crew – Great guys!

to read it over. He finished reading and looked up at the captain and said "Captain, I think this is a dirty rotten trick and very unfair." He handed the report back to the Bull who took it and proceeded to tear it up and said he would rewrite it. He looked over at me and handed me my letter, which I tore up, thanked him, and left his quarters. Not long after that I had another opportunity to read my fitness report that had been greatly altered and very positive. No

Some more of the crew, Chief Yeoman John Criscuolo (upper right) furnished the log of the *Preserver* for me.

more was ever said about it and the issue was closed.

Regarding the captain's relationship with his men, I would like to summarize my observations of the historical role of the captain of a navy ship. When you report aboard a ship you accept the fact that the captain is the supreme authority over all the men under his jurisdiction. A navy ship is an entity unto itself and the captain exerts his authority over all the personnel.

While the ship is under way, every aspect of the crew's behavior and duty is subject to the final decision of the skipper. The captain is responsible for everything that happens to his ship and his men. If any member of the crew or the ship's officers is dissatisfied with his treatment, or the way way the ship is operated, his only recourse is the captain. This is the only way the navy has functioned throughout history and successfully served our country during all our conflicts.

Many years later I received all my records from the navy and I noted in my last fitness report under Captain Hiner the final observation that read as follows:

> *This officer has done fine work as First Lieutenant, and excellent work in salvage operations in Okinawa.*

On August 6, 1945, the first atom bomb was dropped on Hiroshima. This was tremendous news for all of us and significantly hastened the cessation of our war with Japan. Three days later, on August 9th, the second atom bomb was dropped on Nagasaki, and on September 2, Japan formally surrendered. Needless to say we were elated with the great news of the war's final end. No one will ever know

Our Cooks

how many American lives would have been lost in an invasion of Japan.

During this time we had left Pearl Harbor and were on our way to Kwajalein via Johnson Island, a small atoll about 700 miles southwest of Hawaii. When we left Pearl Harbor our assignment was to go to Kwajalein and we had to tow a booster pump barge #2, *YF-756*, and *YF-99*. Accompanying us was the USS *Comorant ATO 133* that was towing *APL-23* and *APL-31*. The *YMS-421* was to be our escort. After we had arrived at Johnson Island the auxiliary tug *Cormorant* had engine trouble and had to dismantle its main engine. In the meantime it became necessary for us to add all the ships that they had been towing to the three that we were towing. So we finally ended up with six vessels in tow including the disabled *Cormorant,* which had lost power. The total length of our tow was now about 4,000 feet and we could only proceed at between three and four knots. Lucky for us the war had just ended, as we would have been a sitting duck for a Japanese submarine. Three days later we finally arrived at Kwajalein and then dropped off our six tows. This was quite a relief as we could now proceed to Guam somewhat faster than three knots.

When we got to Guam we were able to give our crew a day of liberty with a game of softball. They were also eager to partake of a few legal beverages at the enlisted men's club. Oddly enough some of us also quenched our thirsts at the officers' club. After slaking parched throats everybody managed to get back to our ship, but maneuvering up the gangplank was extremely difficult for most of the "four hour" landlubbers. The next day sick bay was quite busy dispensing aspirin and other "mal de mer" meds.

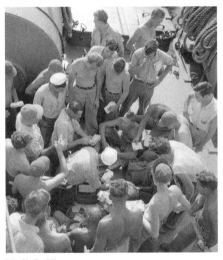

Mail Call!

After we refueled and took on additional provisions we welcomed aboard three marine officers and 20 marines for transportation to Okinawa. It was great for us all to have an opportunity to help some of these wonderful guys who were so instrumental in winning the Pacific war. Unfortunately we did have some rough weather and it was not uncommon to see some of our marine buddies losing their rations over the side.

Six days later we arrived at Buckner Bay, Okinawa, and transferred our 23 marines to their new units on the island. During the next few days about a dozen new enlisted men reported for duty aboard the *Preserver*. On September 29th after seven days at Okinawa we received our orders to proceed to Wakayama, Japan. We were to be a part of the "Guinea Pig Fleet" that would be the first navy ships to sail into the inland sea in Japan. The first part of this fleet included the minesweepers, that were to lead us and clear any mines that had been placed in

Dear Son, ...

the ship lanes. Following the minesweepers there were a number of Liberty ships that only had a skeleton crew aboard in case they struck any mines. The salvage vessels followed the Liberty ships and other navy vessels in the convoy. Whenever the minesweepers would cut a mine loose and it would float to the top we would use our guns to shoot and explode the mines.

Many brave American men rest in Okinawa and didn't get to make the trip back.

Letter to Dad

September 28th, 1945

Dear Dad, LaLa, and all:
Also send this letter to Jim & Barb!

Tonight still finds us in the harbor at Okinawa or Buckner Bay as it is called. We are anchored here and making preparations for a storm due to hit tonight. As a matter of fact one of those typhoons that this area is noted for, is supposed to be on the way.

Fortunately enough we were in Guam several weeks ago when the last typhoon hit. When we arrived here there were quite a few ships on the beach that had dragged anchor or lost their anchors. There was a lot of work to be done and our first job was a beached LST. It was really high and dry but when the tide came in it wasn't too bad but still pretty hard aground. I made a survey of the job with our divers and checked for all the grounding points. Then checked the tide tables and so forth for the best time to pull. Then we removed ammunition, fuel oil and some trucks to lighten it and using two other ships we finally on the third try pulled it off the beach. It was a good job and it was a lot of satisfaction after the work we had done on it. All this work is fun if only your efforts are rewarded and you really accomplish something.

I believe from now on will be a little busier than when we were hanging around Pearl Harbor. Being busy makes the time go much faster and all in all is the best thing for us. There are many ships aground here and I guess quite a few around Japan. As I understand it, in a very short time we are shoving off for Japan to do duty up around there. I don't know exactly when and I believe soon. Sure hope we get a chance to see some of it while we are there as I might as well get my money's worth out of this cruise. We haven't had any chances to get around on Okinawa as we have been pretty busy although I understand there isn't much here anyway. Most of these islands are pretty much the same.

Every new place I see each day that passes makes you realize more and more how wonderful the good old United States is and how lucky we are to live there. Just think how awful it would be to have Mickey and Tommy and all the kids grow up in countries where they have so little chance. Sure would do a lot of good if every American could take a world cruise and finally realize how good it is to be home.

Received LaLa's letter and two from Jim in the past few days and enjoy them immensely as we hadn't any mail since we left Kwajalein about 3 or 4 weeks ago. There's still a lapse of about two weeks for mail that we have some place and should be here soon. Sure was a nice letter LaLa, as I enjoy hearing from you so much. Now that you're a senior you realize how fast school days fly and how fortunate and happy we all were being able to go. It's all something that no one can take away from you as school days are some of the happiest of your life. There so many times when I am thankful for them and realize how small some of the things I worried about were and at times complained. I guess we're all pretty much growing up. The old years are really tumbling by, but we can all look back and realize how happy we have been and will be together no matter how many miles apart we are. The last five years have done a lot but that's inevitable in large families and just knowing that we'll always be together means so much. Jim and Barb's letters were swell and I am very happy to hear that he got stateside assignment near Detroit. The 10 months away from the States is enough for anybody, even one month is enough. Some of these poor kids have done about 20 and when we go to Japan they won't have any immediate hope of returning. I really don't have any idea how long will be there but it doesn't seem logical that it will be anything less than 3-4 months, although I have no definite word. The Navy runs in strange ways. Maybe sometime soon demobilization will catch up with me but there's really no immediate prospects.

Glad you had such a nice Labor Day trip to Canada, Dad, and I think you should do more of that, nothing like the good old out of doors. Another winter is coming around I suppose the old bowling ball will come out of mothballs and you'll be setting the alleys on fire again this year. Is Tommy on the K.C. club yet or is his old man going to do all bowling for the family. I'm dying to see those kids as they must be really sprouting up now. I still haven't heard how Mickey did in school so far but I don't believe he's moved any pianos like his Uncle Jim did. Time sure has flown since that fall when Jim and I were going back to college in Vermont and Mickey was born. The following five years really flew and it won't be long before these kids are grown up.

Football weather should be just beginning and I sure wish I was around to hear the old 'thud' of the pigskin. I believe that next fall will bring back most of the boys and things should be pretty much normal again. There are a great many with enough points but very little transportation to take them back and it just takes time. Maybe I'm just as well-off to not be back during the terrific rush that will follow the first guys looking for jobs and getting back into the swing of life.

Well everyone I guess I'd better hit the sack while it's still calm. Hope you are all well and would like to hear from all my brothers and sister if you get a chance to write. My very best love and kisses to Dad, LaLa, Mike, Tom, Jim, Margaret, Marge, Barb, Mickey, Anne, Carol, the Lees and all.

G 'night for now,

Joe

Wakayama, Honshu, Japan

Before we left Okinawa the weather reports were warning of a typhoon that was approaching and within a day or so would be near this area. We made preparations and on September 29th we were under way to Wakayama, Honshu, Japan. We arrived at Wakayama on October 1st, and made preparations to join the other ships and proceed through the Bungo Straits with

Me – What to do?!

the occupation forces. The weather had been pretty rough and we heard that a major typhoon had struck the area around Okinawa. Coming through the Straits the minesweepers had cut loose some mines and we fired on one but missed it. One of the other ships hit it, however, and it exploded.

We arrived at Hiro Wan near Kobe and anchored for several days. We were quite disappointed that we never set foot on Japan because we were immediately ordered back to Okinawa as the typhoon had caused considerable damage and there were many ships sunk or beached. It was quite frustrating to look through the binoculars and see the people on Honshu and never have an opportunity to go ashore. So on October 12th in the company of a fleet tug we headed back to Okinawa to begin salvage operations. When we arrived at Buckner Bay it was a pretty bad mess. There was a large number of ships on the beaches and the reefs so there was lots of work for us to do.

For the first week or so when we got back to Okinawa we spent most of the time pulling stranded ships off the beach and coral reefs. In some cases it was necessary for our divers to patch the damaged ships before refloating them. October 29th we were ordered to begin operations to refloat the oil transport ship *YOG-80* that was stranded high and dry on a large coral reef at China-Saki, Okinawa. We went aboard the oiler at low tide, checked for damages, and made our plans for refloating her. The typhoon had dropped her off on the reef parallel to the shore and it was obvious that we could not refloat her without a lot of blasting coral and swinging the ship out into a new channel. It was necessary to

Seabees bulldozing coral

prepare the coral reef for blasting in order to create a new channel into which we would swing the bow of the ship. We could only work on the reef during low tide and consequently had to rig tripods to keep the pneumatic hoses out of the water during high tide. Every day Grant and I would go ashore with our crews of divers and we would sink holes in the coral with jackhammers in preparation for blasting. We had made arrangements with Navy Seabees to furnish bulldozers and clear out the loose coral after we had completed blasting. The Seabees were great guys to work with and every day for

Drilling holes in coral for blasting

about 10 days we blasted and they cleared the channel in the coral so we could swing the ship 90 degrees toward the open sea.

One night as it was getting dark and the tide was coming in, we proceeded as usual back to the dock to get a lift out to our ship that was anchored in the harbor. Generally we could get a lift from one of the small boats that were going in and out to the ships at anchor. On this particular day after blasting and working in the hot sun with the Seabees we were all pretty pooped and ready to get back to the *Preserver.* I noticed one guy who seemed to be in charge of one of the boats and I said, " Hey bud, hows' about giving us a lift out to the *Preserver.*" He kind of snarled, and said, " Is that the way you speak to a senior officer?" I looked a little closer, and

Passing Tow Line

sure enough on his cap there was an eagle. Somewhat pissed off, I mumbled an apology and needless to say we didn't get a lift with him out to the ship. Once in awhile you could get some officer who was impressed by his rank but under those circumstances his attitude stunk. The Salvage Navy was always a lot less formal as we were divers like the enlisted men and always worked very close with the guys on most operations. Spit-and-polish was the least of our worries.

After many days of blasting and bulldozing the loose coral, we were about ready to start pulling the stranded ship off the beach. On

November 19th, at low tide, we ran towing wire out to the YOG and prepared to commence pulling. When the tide came in our skipper ordered the ship "full speed ahead," and the tow line was pulled taut. With several of these yanks the bow of the ship swung out into the channel that we had dug and faced the open sea. All that remained now was to reset our tow lines to the

Finally it floats!

bow and pull her out to sea.

We secured for the day and prepared to come in at the next high tide and finish towing the ship through the channel and free of the reef. The next morning at high tide we heaved on our tow to the YOG and moved it about 3 ft. At low tide the bilge keel had to be cut off as it had jammed under the ship and was hindering forward movement. The fleet tug *ATF 152* reported to assist and her tow wire was passed to the *YOG 80*. The *ATA 186* also reported to assist and her tow wire was passed to our bow in order to tow in tandem. At evening high tide towing commenced and after forward movements of 15 feet, 10 feet, and 10 more feet the *YOG 80* slid free of the coral reef and was afloat at 18:45. The ATF's tow line was castoff the *YOG 80*. We inspected all the compartments and tanks on the oiler and all were watertight. We heaved the *YOG 80* short on the tow wire and anchored for the night.

The next day we were all elated at the success of the operation, and towed the ship out. It was the first time she was at anchor since the typhoon. In those days "high fives" were not in vogue, but we all shook hands at the success of our efforts. I knew our skipper, the Bull, was pleased, but he generally had a tough time expressing praise.

No Lettuce!

One day while we were taking on provisions the captain went over to the supply ship as he had a close friend who was one of the supply officers. Not long after he came aboard he announced that he had secured a case of fresh lettuce. Now one thing we never had aboard the *Preserver* was fresh lettuce. It was something you never missed

The Captain

until you found out it wasn't ever going to be available. We thought that was a pretty good deal and looked forward to a fresh salad for our next meal. However, Capain Hiner had other ideas about his case of lettuce.

The next meal the stewards mate brought in a nice big chunk of lettuce to the captain with a gob of thousand island dressing. He proceeded to dig into it with no mention of sharing any of it with us. Nobody said anything and we proceeded to eat our chow without any of that scrumptious lettuce. There was not much we could do but we got together and decided to give the captain the old silent treatment. For the next few days nobody spoke to the old man unless he spoke to us. The only responses he got from us were "Yes, captain," "No, captain," and "Aye, Aye Sir." I guess he got the message but we still didn't get any lettuce.

On December 10th Chief Warrant Officer W. C. Brosey received orders to be transferred back to the States. Brosey and I had become real close friends. As first lieutenant on the ship I worked quite closely with him, together with the deck crew whose chief petty officer was a sailor named Hogan.

Hogan was one of those guys who if you wanted something done he was always ready, willing, and able to comply.

Lots of nights after chow, when we were under way Brosey would say to me, "Joey, let's go out on the front porch and have a cigar." So we'd go up on the bow, sit and talk, and watch the sun disappear into the beautiful Pacific Ocean. I was going to miss those nights with my old pal Brosey. He was one of the great old Mustangs who spent his whole life in the navy, served all over the globe, and was finally going back to retirement. This was an old timer who didn't resent "90-day wonders."

Sometime in early November when we were in Okinawa I got the word that I was being promoted from Lt. (jg) to the rank of full lieutenant. Captain Hiner, having been notified of this by the Bureau of Personnel, wrote me the following letter:

From: The Commanding Officer

To: Lt. jg Joseph E. Corbett

Subject: Notification of Appointment

1. All stipulated conditions having been fulfilled your appointment to the rank of lieutenant, for temporary service, made by the President on November 1, 1945, to rank from November 1, 1945, is delivered. Your BuPers file number is 255201.

C. B. Hiner

I was quite pleased by this after having gone through some pretty rough times early on after his arrival as captain. Nothing more was ever discussed about our first conversation and after having gone through all our work in Okinawa, I guess the captain had changed his mind about salvage officers.

Heading Home – Finally!

We were kept busy for several weeks more in the Okinawa area. Then we received orders to proceed to Guam then on to Hawaii. When we got to Guam we were assigned the task of towing a disabled ship all the way back to Hawaii. Salvage vessels aren't the speediest ships in the Navy and when you have a fairly heavy ship in tow, the average speed is somewhere around 10 knots.

We reached the epitome of monotony on that trip to Hawaii. The deck crew could just chip so much paint as we kept trying to keep everybody busy. We did have some fun every once in a while having some jam sessions in Grant's and my room. I had a little plastic flute that the U.S.O. had given us, Grant had a gallon jug that he could play, and Hal Timmerman had a couple of castanets made out of old light bulbs. We would get together and knock off a few choruses of "Rum and Coca Cola" – without the rum. Every once in a while the Bull, our skipper, would stick his head into the room and scowl. His appreciation for good music was sadly lacking.

We also had a light punching bag rigged up on the aft part of the ship. I used to go out every afternoon and smash the hell out of that bag. Now that the war was over all anybody could think about was going home.

At the speed we were going, it took quite some time to get to Hawaii. The guys on the ship were looking forward to their first liberty in Honolulu. A very important thing was to get your white uniform as white as possible. The guys spent their spare time dragging their whites in back of the ship so they could really bleach out.

Finally we were getting close to Hawaii and everybody was pretty charged up about getting back on "terra firma." We were pretty well squared away about the various liberty crews and who would go over for the first shore leave. Grant, who was doing the navigating, had figured out pretty well when we would arrive.

The first look you get of Oahu is to see Diamond Head looming up over the horizon – a really welcome sight for most of the guys after being away for so long. We called the harbor master, reported in and got our dock assignment in Pearl Harbor. The first group of guys to go ashore was the starboard group and they were raring to go. They were spic n'span in their whites as they saluted the Officer Of the Deck (OOD), and took off for their first liberty in a long time.

Most of the officers stayed aboard as we had plenty to do getting everything ready and reporting our arrival. I was grabbing a quick nap in my sack for a couple of hours when the OOD called and said that I had a phone call. It hadn't been more than two or three hours after the first liberty crew had gone ashore. However the phone call was from Bosn's Mate Hogan. He was calling from a phone booth in downtown Honolulu and seemed to be in some distress. He said he had lost his pants and I'd better come and get him because he couldn't run around in just his shorts. I jumped into the jeep and whipped down to the phone booth and there he was, somewhat disheveled and minus his pants. Fortunately I was driving as Hogan was in no shape to take the wheel. Back to the ship we went. I winked at the OOD and got Hogan into his sack. So much for his first shore leave.

The next day Bob Matthews and I decided to get a hotel room at the Moana Hotel on Waikiki beach so we could go for swim, have a some meals and a few drinks on shore. Those were relaxing days, a wonderful relief after the monotony of the long trip from Okinawa. After a couple of drinks and a great dinner, the cocktail hour was resumed for quite some time. We did get to hit the sack in a couple of comfortable beds but the next day we were both a little "shore-sick" when we reported back to the *Preserver*.

Sometime later we received the news that we were assigned to take part in the atom bomb tests on Bikini Island. We were to report to San Francisco, however, until such time as the Bikini tests were to take place. About this time I knew I had sufficient points to be discharged from the navy and was looking forward to that great day of liberation. We were soon issued orders to proceed back to the States via San Diego and then San Francisco. The crew was ecstatic about orders to return home and immediately began preparing the home-coming pennant to be flown when we left Hawaii. One day on the way back Captain Hiner called me to his cabin. When I got there he was quite cordial and informed me that I had sufficient points to get out of the navy. He said, however, "I was hoping that you would stay with us for the atom bomb tests." This surprised me but I said, "I'm sorry Captain, I want to go home." With that our conversation ended, we shook hands, and I left his cabin.

San Francisco / New York / Buffalo

It wasn't long before the *Preserver* received orders to proceed to San Diego and then San Francisco. Without the need to tow another vessel we were able to head for the States alone. This was a great relief as we could proceed at our own speed and get back home as quickly as possible. The trip was uneventful and we arrived in San Diego around a week later. It was our first time back to the States and we were all looking forward to San Francisco, the final leg of our trip.

After refueling and taking on more supplies we took off for San Francisco. Several days later we had the city in sight and proceeded into the bay under the Golden Gate Bridge. Naturally this was a sight for sore eyes because this was the symbol of coming home much like the Statue of Liberty was when we came back from Europe. About that time we received the following communication from the Director of Dispersal 12.

From: DIRDISPERSTWELVE
Action: CO USS PRESERVE
Info: SEPCEN SFRAN CALIF
BUT PERS
COMSERVPAC

ACCORDANCE ALNAV L98- 1945 WHEN DIRECTED BY CO FOLLOWING OFFICERS DETACHED PRESENT DUTY SUCH OTHER DUTIES ASSIGNED PROCEED IMMEDIATELY CO SEPCEN DESIGNATED DUTY PENDING RELEASE TO INACTIVE DUTY

ACCORDANCE PROVISIONS ALNAV 76-46 X NECESSARY FUR-
NISH 25 COPIES ORDERS X LT JOSEPH EDWARD CORBETT S[E]
USNR 255201 TO SEPCEN NYK X LTJG GRANT ANDERSON HAR-
RIS D USNR 394258 AND ENS HAROLD WAYNE TIMMERMAN D
USNR 404052 TO SEPCEN 703 MARKET ST SFRAN CALIF X

The next endorsement was as follows;

> *USS Preserver ARS 8*
> *C/O Fleet Post Office*
> *San Francisco, Calif*
> *2 April 1946*
> *From: Commanding Officer*
> *To: Lieut. Joseph Edward Corbett, S{E},USNR*
> *Subject: Change Of Duty*
> *Ref: {A} Above Dispatch.*
> *1. In Accordance with Reference {A} You Are Hereby Detached This*
> *Date.*
> *Proceed And Carry Out Basic Orders.*
> *C. B. Hiner*

This was the kind of communication we were all waiting for. In classic navy fashion they sent me all the way to New York to be separated while Grant and Tim were separated in San Francisco. The three of us said our good byes to all our shipmates. It was not without a lump in our throats that we left the *Preserver* after so many days of lasting friendships. I spent a day with Tim, Grant, and his family, and took off for New York.

Air transportation was not available at that time because so many servicemen and women were heading home. So I got a sleeper out of San Francisco and took off on my last navy trip. The train trip to New York was a lot of fun because many of us were heading home. It was a continuous rolling party until we got to New York.

I reported on April 7, 1946, had my physical and was detached on the ninth of April. I had accumulated leave of one month and 25 days that expired on June 3, 1946. I took the train back to Buffalo to my wonderful family. I sure missed mother.

I was in the Navy 3 years, 2 months and 17 days.

The Postwar Years

After I got out of the service in June of 1946, I returned to North Tonawanda and moved back home with my dad and my sister Loretta. As with all the other veterans, my next question was, "What am I going to do with the rest of my life?" I had my mechanical engineering degree, so college was not my normal next step. Most of my friends right after they were discharged either entered college, looked for a job, or applied for unemployment insurance – and took their time seeking a job. I seriously considered applying to law school. Using my G.I. Bill to get a law degree to combine with my engineering degree made a lot of sense as it seemed like a great combination.

My dad was not a great believer in federal handouts, discouraging me from loafing around and drinking beer with all my buddies. Law school intrigued me but after three and a half years in the navy I decided I'd better get a job and get on with my career.

I grew up peddling papers, selling magazines, working in drug and grocery stores, so a sales career appealed to me. Engineering related sales seemed to be a logical choice so I began looking for that type of work.

After answering a few ads and interviewing for several jobs I accepted a position with the Gates Rubber Company from Denver, Colorado, as a field engineer. This work entailed traveling all over western New York and calling on any kind of an industrial plant that could conceivably use the Gates products. Their major products were industrial V- belts and pulleys. They also specialized in custom-made molded rubber products. The work was very interesting. I had the opportunity of calling on a very large segment of manufacturing firms.

After about a year and a half my boss, Lee Witzenburg, called me into his office and told me he was accepting a job as sales manager for a major diecasting company in Detroit. After having worked as a branch manager for Gates Rubber the opportunity to be a national sales manager was a welcome challenge for him. He described his new responsibility with the Congress Die Casting company and offered me a job covering the state of Michigan and several adjoining states.

The possibilities of this new job offer were very appealing as coincidentally my brother Jim had recently moved to Lansing, Michigan, as a sales engineer for the Spaulding Fibre Company. I accepted the new job, left Gates Rubber and moved to Lansing to reside with my brother Jim and his family. While in Lansing I became acquainted with George Nelson and Fred Nattare, who were students at Michigan State College. George, from Lutsen, Minnesota, was an ardent skier and we spent many weekends driving to Boyne Mountain in upper Michigan. He had a nice Studebaker car and we had great times skiing the Michigan "mountains."

After a few months I decided it would be more convenient to live in Detroit and soon moved to the Motor City. Answering an ad I moved to a boarding house in the Indian Village section of Detroit. There were about a dozen other guys, mostly vets, living in Ma Hutto's boarding house. It was a great group of fellows from all over the country, many of them with sales jobs with other manufacturing businesses in the Detroit area. I soon made a lot of new friends as we had much in common and did a great amount of socializing. Because a good number of them were in sales, we could quite often plan on being in the same cities on our sales trips. In many respects it was like living in a fraternity house except we were somewhat more mature, having all had recent experiences in the service.

After some time a group of us decided we would like to live in a suburb of Detroit and rent an apartment. Eight of us therefore moved to the lovely town of Birmingham, north of Detroit. We rented a nice apartment in a complex on 13 Mile Road. My roommates were Art Zerbey, Jud Decker, and Dick McKenzie. Art was from New York, Jud from Kansas, and Dick from Massachusetts. The other group of four living across the street from us were Jim Page, Jack McCrehan, George Cantrick, and Paul Haefner. We were all graduates of Ma Hutto's.

These were great years and we had wonderful times skiing and hunting in northern Michigan, watching the Detroit Tigers, the Lions and the Red Wings. In the fall we had Saturday trips to watch Michigan and Michigan State football games.

Inevitably wedding bells began to break up that "old gang of mine." Art, Jud, George, Craig, and Jack got married, and Dick moved to Vermont.

I had just heard from my good friend George Little in Burlington, Vermont, and he had asked me if I might be interested in moving back to Burlington and joining him in a business venture. I always had a secret desire to get back to Vermont as I loved the country and the people, but engineering jobs were not too abundant in the Green Mountains. We both flew to New York to discuss our partnership. George had been working for the *Burlington Free Press* in their commercial printing division called Champlain printers. We discussed the possibilities in which my function would be the sales end of the business and George would be in the production end. George had a great graphic arts background as his father had been running the Champlain Printing Company and George had a graduate degree in printing from the University of Pittsburgh.

I knew virtually nothing about the printing business but I had a lot of experience in sales. It didn't take me long to make my decision. I quit my job in Detroit, packed up my car, and moved to Burlington in 1950.

Detroit Friends in World War II

James R. Conant – U.S.Navy
Cambridge, Massachusetts

I met Jim Conant in 1947 when I started working in Detroit and moved into Ma Hutto's boarding house in Indian Village. He had just arrived in Detroit after working for the *Boston Globe* for several years. His new job was with *Time* magazine, as their Assistant Bureau Chief.

Jim came from Cambridge, Massachusetts, where his father, James Bryan Conant, was President of Harvard University and head of the National Defense Research Committee guiding the nation's scientific and technical programs. Shunning the Ivy schools, Jim had decided to go to the University of Michigan. He had attended Phillips Andover Academy and then on to Ann Arbor where he graduated from U of M at the age of 19. Quiet and unassuming but smart as hell, Jim soon became a good friend of all of us. After about a year in Detroit he was transferred to the Chicago office of *Time* magazine. I made several pilgrimages to Chicago and spent some weekends with Jim. He had a nice apartment in the center of Chicago but his culinary acumen was sadly lacking. I looked in his refrigerator and all he had was a bottle of Maraschino cherries and a bag of potato chips. Needless to say we frequented a few Chicago restaurants.

One year another friend of mine, Dick McKenzie, and I joined Jim for a ski vacation in Sun Valley, Idaho. Jim was something less than a superb athlete but we had a great time skiing real mountains with lots of snow.

Around 1950 he was transferred to Montreal, Quebec where he was the bureau chief for *Time* magazine until 1957. After I moved to Vermont in 1950, Jim and I got together quite often in Burlington and Montreal. When I married Mae in 1952, Jim came down to our wedding. In later years he was chief editorial writer for the *Baltimore News American* and also did freelance work for many publications including *Atlantic* magazine. He retired in 1979, and passed away in 1982.

During those years none of us discussed very much about our World War II experiences. I knew Jim was in the submarine service but was never aware of any details of his experiences. I eventually contacted Jim's brother, Theodore, who was living in New York City. He was kind enough to fill me in on some of the details, which were covered in the book *Take Her Deep* written by Admiral I. J. Galantin, USN, who was the skipper of the submarine *Halibut SS 232* on which Jim served from 1943-1945.

In 1943 Jim volunteered for the U.S. Navy, requesting submarine service. He went through his training in sub school at New London and his first assignment was the *Halibut SS 232*. He reported to the *Halibut* while she was in Pearl Harbor in November of 1943 after returning from patrols in the Aleutians and the northeast coast of Japan. In the newly constituted "wolf pack" technique the *Halibut* was assigned to a group with two other subs, the *Tullibee* and the *Haddock*. This group departed from Pearl Harbor on December 14th headed for Midway to fuel up to the maximum for the unknown number of days ahead. When they arrived in Midway, Jim and Joseph Galligan, another new officer, were summoned to visit the Division Commander, Captain Carl G. Hensel. The captain asked Jim where he had gone to school. Jim replied, "University of Michigan." The next question was, "What did you major in?" Jim answered, "Philosophy." The captain's eyebrows arched and they could see that was not considered a good answer. He then turned to Joe to ask him the same questions and he answered, "Holy Cross, and Economics," answers that did not impress the commander. He said, "I don't know what's happening back there. Last week they sent me a grave digger." But he added "Good luck, anyway."

Referring to Jim in his book Galantin says,

> *Jim was a gangling six-footer, who never gained weight even though he was a prodigious eater. Whether seated or afoot, he had an atrocious posture. He seemed to be all elbows and knees, about to fly apart at any*

moment. If I was in the cramped space of the bridge when Jim had the deck I took care to avoid being bumped off the upper level as he shuffled restlessly about. And when he yelled, "Clear the bridge! Dive! Dive!" it was every man for himself. Whoever was ahead of him as his rawboned frame came hurtling down the hatch, quickly learned to get out of the way.

It was clear that sports had not been much of a factor in Jim's young life. There was no smooth coordination of muscle to match the elegance of his mind. Still by the time we reached our patrol area I knew I had another alert, competent, trustworthy officer of the deck.

After Midway the three ships turned to the west and proceeded with 15 miles between ships. Crossing the date line they skipped December 20th and advanced their clocks to December 21st. They were proceeding through a heavy storm causing the ships to pitch heavily. In the strong gale winds reached speed up to 45 knots, and they were riding waves averaging 20 to 50 feet. Soon the storm abated and they were able to enjoy a Christmas dinner. The crew's mess room and the wardroom were festooned with tinsel and familiar Christmas ornaments that Commissary Officer Jim Conant had obtained in Pearl Harbor.

Twenty-four hours later about a hundred miles southeast of Marcus Island the aircraft warning radar indicated a plane 8 miles and closing. "Clear the bridge! Dive! Dive!" shouted the officer of the deck. He and the three lookouts landed in the control room with great thumps. They immediately transmitted to the Wolf pack, "Diving for plane", to warn the other two submarines. Leveling off at about 150-foot depth three bombs exploded, not close enough to cause damage but loud enough to tell all hands that we were in enemy territory. On December 30, when speaking to the Tullibee, they were saddened to learn that a huge wave had crushed one of her lookouts against the guard rail with such force that his binoculars were jammed into his diaphragm. He was carried below in great pain and torpedo man, Lawrence Kidwell. died that night of internal injuries and was given a sailor's burial.

After their eighth patrol they returned to Midway on February 2, 1944.

The *Halibut* departed on her ninth patrol on March 21, 1944. Cruising eastward of Okinawa she sank passenger cargo ship TAICHU MARU, and fired six torpedoes to separate a convoy on April 27th. Closing in on a ship separated from the group, *Halibut* sank GENBU MARU, then shifted her attack to coastal mine layer KANOME sinking her also. She was then forced into evasive action as some 90 depth charges were dropped close aboard. Surfacing off the northeastern shore of Kume Shima, she bombarded two ware- houses and other buildings with her deck gun and made an attack on a group of sampans with gunfire on May 3rd. With men critical- ly wounded in the gun battle she returned to Pearl Harbor May 15, 1944. She then sailed for overhaul to San Francisco and returned to Hawaii on September 20, 1944.

On her tenth war patrol *Halibut* again joined a coordinated attack group, this time with *Haddock* and *Tuna*. While proceeding to Luzon Strait, the submarines were ordered to set up scouting lines to inter- cept crippled units of the Japanese fleet retiring after the battle off Cape Engano. It encountered the remnants of Admiral Ozawa's force October 25, and attacked, inflicting some damage. The sub's next contact came November 14, when she attacked a convoy in Luzon Strait. She was immediately attacked by planes apparently using magnetic airborne detectors. A short but effective depth charge attack directed by the aircraft left *Halibut* severely damaged but still under control. Her crew made temporary repairs and she steamed into Saipan on November 19. The gallant submarine received a Navy Unit Commendation for her performance on this patrol.

On December 1, 1944 *Halibut* passed the sea buoy marking the channel leading into Pearl Harbor. In Captain Galantin's words, "Jim Conant had the deck. I had only to keep a watchful eye and careful ear to his orders as he skillfully conned our ship alongside." ComSubPacs band assembled on the dock and sounded off with "The Stars and Stripes Forever."

Halibut had brought her crew safely home. She was a proud unit of a force that had lost 22 percent of the people it sent on war patrol.

Halibut returned to Portsmouth, New Hampshire, January 16, 1945, where it was found that her damage was too extensive to justify repair. She was decommissioned on July 18, 1945 and sold for scrap to Quaker shipyard. The United States Treasury received a check for $23,123.

Jim Conant had served honorably aboard this great fighting ship, receiving a number of decorations including the Silver Star. It was a privilege to have had him as a friend.

A. Craig Edmunds – U.S. Navy

Lowell, Massachusetts

Craig was one of my Detroit friends that I met skiing at Boyne Mountain in Northern Michigan. He was a sales engineer with the Square D Company and we had similar jobs calling on many of the major industries in the Michigan area. We

Craig Edmunds   did a lot of skiing together in northern Michigan and a fair amount of socializing. When Craig jumped off the deep end and got married to a lovely gal, Marion Stone, I was his best man.

We swapped a lot of World War II sea stories as Craig had served on the USS *Higbee* in the Asian Theater.

He joined the navy on December 15, 1942, as an apprentice seaman and went to boot camp at Newport, Rhode Island, then to Class A fire control school in Newport and to advanced fire control school at Annacosta, District of Columbia. He then had a special assignment on the Mark 50 director project. His first sea duty assignment was, in April 1945, to the destroyer *Higbee, DD 806*, a Gearing Class ship named after Lenah Higbee, who had been the chief of the Navy Nurse Corps during World War I. It was the first U.S. Navy ship named after a real woman.

Under the command of Commander Lindsay Williamson, the *Higbee* was converted to a radar picket destroyer. Craig reported to the ship in April of 1945 and on May 24th she joined the famed Carrier Task Force 38 less than 40 miles from Tokyo Bay. "Leaping Lenah," as she had been dubbed by her crew, screened the carriers as their planes launched heavy air attacks against the Japanese mainland until the end of hostilities on August 15th. While screening the carriers, the *Higbee* knocked down four enemy airplanes and after the war ended destroyed two more. She helped clear Japanese minefields and supported the occupation forces for the following seven months, finally returning to San Diego in April 1946.

Craig was discharged from the service on June 13th 1946 as a fire controlman second-class. He had earned the American Theater, Asiatic Theater with one Star, Japanese Occupation, Philippine Liberation, World War II, Victory, and Good Conduct medals.

We get together with Craig and Stoney several times a year and helped him celebrate their 50th wedding anniversary in 2001 at their home in Franconia, N.H.

Arthur Zerbey – U.S. ARMY AIR CORPS
Greenwich. Connecticut

Art Zerbey was one of the fellows I met at Ma Hutto's boarding house in Detroit. He graduated from Yale University and was working for the Island Creek Coal Company in their sales department. He was one of the eight who moved to Birmingham, Michigan, and lived with Jud Decker, Dick McKenzie, and me in a condominium. I think he was probably the only Yale graduate who ever wanted to be in the coal business. Whoever heard of a guy that sang the "Whiffenpoof Song" from "the tables down at Mory's" becoming a coalman – anyway Art was a great guy and is still one of my best friends. When he married his dear wife Nancy in 1949 I was his best man. They reside in Naples, Florida where we get together every year and play some golf. He continues to beat me.

Right after he graduated from Yale in 1943 he joined the Air Force. After six months' training in the United States he was sent to England to a Base Air Depot, as an electrical specialist for two years

– then for six months in Munich in a Troop Carrier Command C-47s as a staff sergeant. He returned to the states and was discharged in 1946. Like all of us he was "glad, glad, glad" to see the end of it.

James H. O. Page – U.S. ARMY AIR FORCE
New Britain, Connecticut

Jim Page was one of my roommates in Detroit, Michigan, in 1947. He was a salesman for a tool company calling on many of the major car manufacturers. He was a little younger than most of us and enlisted in the Army Air Corps on November 16, 1943. He was initially a B-24 aircraft mechanic and then a B-24 flight engineer. He was then transferred to the B-29 program as an aircraft mechanic and then the cadet program to be a B-29 flight engineer/cruise control specialist. Before his B-29 training program was completed the war ended. He was discharged November 7, 1945.

Jim now lives in Florida and we get together and play golf during our annual Florida winter vacation. We still have reunions with several of our old Detroit buddies.

George Cantrick – NAVAL AIR FORCE
Monroe, Michigan

George Cantrick was one of the group of eight guys who lived with us in Birmingham, Michigan, in 1947-49. He was from Monroe, Michigan, and went to college in Ohio. In January of 1943 he volunteered for the Navy Air Force and trained in torpedo bombers at Pensacola. After receiving his wings he was assigned to the Naval Air Base on Palmyra Island, a thousand miles south of Hawaii. One of the Line Islands, this base helped to control extensive areas of the central Pacific. The TBF Avenger was a torpedo bomber and flew off carriers and the airfield at Palmyra. George flew torpedo missions during his extended duty on Palmyra. He was discharged in January of 1946 as a lieutenant and returned to his Michigan home.

I first met him in 1948 when I moved to Detroit. We were great friends during these years and I was in the wedding party when he married his wife, Pat. We have kept in close touch in Michigan, Vermont, and during our winter visits to Florida. George was an avid sailor and with his four sons participated in many of the Detroit-to-Mackinaw Island annual races. George's son Chris was a member of the Oracle team which competed in the America's Cup competition in New Zealand. One year we had a reunion on Mackinaw Island and Art Zerbey, Jack McCrehan, and I joined George on his sailboat, *Scarlet Fever*, and we spent a wonderful week sailing the North Channel in Upper Lake Huron. Sadly George passed away in 1999. We still see Pat on our Florida visits and had a reunion with Pat, the Zerbeys and Jim Page in February 2002.

John McCrehan – U.S. NAVY
Lake Wylie, South Carolina

Jack McCrehan and I first met at Ma Hutto's boarding house in Detroit and he was one of the group that lived in Birmingham. Jack went to Colgate University and then entered the navy on the second of September, 1943. He was assigned to duty in the amphibious forces and subsequently was assigned to the *LCT 1298*. In October of 1943 they participated in the operations in Leyte Gulf. During this Philippines campaign he was wounded by shrapnel and was awarded the Purple Heart. He was discharged on March 31, 1946. During the past few years we have been in close contact with Jack and his wife Phyllis and visited them at their Lake Wylie home. He passed away several years ago.

Judson Decker – U.S. ARMY
Birmingham, Michigan

Jud Decker was another one of my Detroit friends who lived with us in Birmingham, Michigan. He was working for *Time/Life* in sales for their advertising division. During the time we lived together Jud dated and fell in love with a lovely girl, Jane Bopp. It wasn't long before they decided to get married and Jud took instructions and converted to Roman Catholicism. When he was baptized, Jane asked me to be his godfather, and I was happy to be so honored. When it came time for his baptism, we appeared in the old Catholic church in Birmingham for the ceremony. It is customary at some point during the ceremony for the godfather to hold the baby in his arms. Jud was about six foot two and almost 200 pounds, so I just placed my hand on the little tyke's head.

Oddly enough, during those years, none of us talked very much about World War II, although we all knew everyone had participated. I guess the general attitude was that we all had gone through it and pretty much decided to go on with our lives and put it in the past. We all went in different directions. Jud stayed in Detroit and I ended up in Burlington, Vermont. Jud and Jane founded the Bopp-Decker Plastic Company, which made some of the first insulated plastic dinnerware. This was sold in grocery stores as promotional items. After 17 years, the business was sold and Jud became a stock-broker and an industrial real-estate salesman. He retired in 1989.

He passed away in June 10, 2002, and I have since been in touch with Jane and his daughter, Sue Philbin. Sue has given me information on Jud's World War II record that I have been able to further supplement from a book, *See Naples And Die*, by Robert Ellis, one of his close friends in the U.S. Army 10th Mountain Division.

Jud was born in Lincoln, Nebraska, on August 15th, 1924. He had enrolled in and was attending Princeton University when the war broke out. He volunteered for the U.S. Army ski troops and entered the service in April of 1943. His first orders were assignment to the Mountain Training Center, Camp Hale in Pando, Colorado, for basic training. At this time he first met and became close friends with Bob Ellis. In July Jud was assigned to Company A of the 85th Division while his friend Bob was assigned to Company F. In June of 1944 they were ordered to Camp Swift in Austin, Texas, and would be there until December of that year. On January 4, 1944, they left Newport News, Virginia, on the USS *West Point* and learned their destination was Naples, Italy. Nine days later they arrived in Naples Harbor, Italy. They then disembarked and marched 3 miles to 16 waiting Landing Craft Infantry. Thirty hours later they landed in Leghorn (Livorno), Italy, disembarked, and bivouacked in a field outside Pisa, the staging area.

The 85th Division with the 87th and 86th took and held Mount Belvedere in this most significant Apennine victory. In one of the passages in Ellis's book, *See Naples And Die*, he writes:

> As we passed through the first Battalion lines to relieve their attacking elements, I met my old friend, Jud Decker, returning down the trail with others in his company. With some trepidation, I greeted him but we only had time for a brief exchange. "How has it been?" I asked. "Boy, am I glad to see you" Jud answered. "In fact, I'm glad to be able to say, "I'm glad to see you. It's been pure hell, and I'm afraid you'll find it just as bad."

The 10th mountain division continued down to the Po Valley and to the final combat in the vicinity of Lake Garda.

On July 31, 1945, the 85th Division boarded the *Marine Fox of Liberty* ship that was to transport them back to the States. On August 10, 1945, they arrived in New York Harbor.

Jud Decker was honorably discharged as a first sergeant on January 25, 1946. He returned to Princeton to earn his degree in Economics and graduated in 1949. I will always cherish my memories of Jud, my biggest godson.

George U. Nelson – 10TH MOUNTAIN
Lutsen, Minnesota

In 1947, I first moved to Michigan and lived in Lansing with my brother Jim and his family. I did a lot of skiing at Boyne Mountain in northern Michigan and during that time I met George Nelson who was a student at Michigan State. During the winter months on most weekends we would pile into George's Studebaker and drive up to Boyne. Skiing was not new to George, whose family ran the Lutsen ski resort in northern Minnesota.

He was an excellent skier and on September 10, 1943, he volunteered and joined the ski troops. He was in Company C, 85th

Regiment, 10th Mountain Division. They had mountain training at Camp Hale, Colorado, from October 1943 to June of 1944. He then went to Camp Swift, Texas, from June to December 1944.

The division entered combat on January 28, 1945, in the North Apennine Mountains of Italy. The division faced German positions arrayed along the 5-mile long Monte Belvedere/Mont della Torracio Ridge. Other divisions had attempted to assault Mont Belvedere three times, even holding it temporarily, but none had succeeded. After assaulting and taking Riva Ridge the division assaulted Mont Belvedere next. It was heavily manned and protected with mine-fields. Several regiments made a bayonet attack with covering artillery fire. The surprise assault was successful and after a hard fight, the peak was captured. On April 14, 1945, the final phase of the war in Italy began. After 110 days of combat, of George's original 12-man squad, 3 were killed, 4 wounded, 4 were unhurt. George contracted pneumonia and on April 14th went to the regional hospital for 3 weeks. From May until July 1945 they were in the occupation forces in Italy. He then returned to the States until his discharge in January 1946 as a PFC.

George noted in his letter to me:

I was one of the lucky ones. My calculations are 7,000 infantry, 4,000 to 5,000 support troops, in the 10th. Out of these infantry 998 were killed and 4,154 wounded. Works out to 70% killed or wounded in 110 days of combat. Take this ratio for an extended time in the infantry and the chances of making it go to zero; either killed, wounded, captured, or transferred. Thank God the war ended. Respectfully, George

His wife Patti added a note for this book;

In March, George returned to northern Italy with seven of his combat comrades of Company C, 85th Reg. 10th Mtn Div, of World War II. They visited the battleground of small mountain villages in the Apennine Mountains and the Po Valley. They found several of their foxholes where they had 'dug in' 53 years ago. A very emotional and interesting experience.

George epitomized the soldiers of the famed 10th Mountain Division in World War II. They fought hard and distinguished themselves in the valiant and crucial battles in Italy.

After the war George returned home and entered college at Michigan State University in Lansing, Michigan. It was at this time that I first met George and we began a long close friendship. After college he returned to Lutsen, Minnesota, where the family ran the Lutsen Resort and ski area. He married Patti and they raised three daughters and one son. Their daughter, Cindy Nelson, was to become a great Olympic skier. She was the first U.S. skier to win the World Cup downhill in 1974, U.S. Alpine skier of the year '75, '76, '78, and '79, and won the Bronze Medal in the '76 Olympic Games.

Veterans of the 10th Mountain Division are in large part responsible for the development of skiing into a big name sport and popular vacation industry after World War II. Ex-soldiers from the 10th laid out ski hills, built ski lodges, designed ski lifts, and improved ski equipment. They started ski magazines and opened ski schools. Vail, Aspen, Stowe, Sugarbush, Lutsen, Crystal Mountain, and Whiteface Mountain are but of a few of the ski resorts in which 10th Mountain veterans participated in their success.

Some time ago George and Patti visited us in Burlington, Vermont, on a skiing vacation to Stowe. We hope some day soon to visit them in Lutsen and play a round of golf on their great resort course.

Back to Vermont

Burlington, Vermont

Returning to Burlington was one of my most cherished dreams and now it was being fulfilled. I came back in 1950 and immediately got my total immersion and exposure to the printing business. George Little had arranged the purchase of an existing lithography business he had been working with for some time. His father George Sr. had been operating the company as

Champlain Printers, a division of the *Burlington Free Press.* We pretty much divided the responsibilities between sales and production, I handled the sales, and George the production.

One of our major clients was the University of Vermont. During the course of our relationship with the university I met a lovely young lady who was the Secretary to Dean Robert Kroepsch. She was the one! Mae Johnson and I were married on November 15, 1952. This year 2002 marked our 50th anniversary.

Mr. & Mrs Joseph E. Corbett

Mae's parents – Nina & Henry L. Johnson

Henry L. Johnson in WWI

Christmas 2001

A short time after we were married, Mae's mother and father moved from Albany to Burlington after he retired. It was good and enjoyable to have her folks closer by. Mae's father, Henry Johnson served in the United States Army during World War I.

During our years of marriage we have been fortunate enough to have four wonderful young sons, who have married four terrific daughters in-law, and given us ten grandchildren – four girls and six boys.

Three of our boys, Joe, Bruce, and Ned live in Vermont while Peter is living right across the border in Shutesbury, Massachusetts.

Joe is a practicing neurosurgeon and lives in Pittsford, Vermont. His wife Jean gave birth to triplets, Joe, Jim and John. Jeffrey arrived a year and a half later. All the boys are hockey players and keep their folks busy getting to practices and games.

Bruce and Maureen live in Hinesburg, Vermont. They have two lovely daughters, Rachel and Julie, who are in college. Bruce studied biomedical photography at RIT and was recently manager of the digital imaging department at the Capital City Press. Photography is his trade and he enjoys shooting photomicrographs of actual snowflakes. Maureen is an R.N. and works in the Labor & Delivery Department at the Fletcher Allen Medical Center hospital.

Peter is married to Jill Cohen and they are both Psychologists. They have two children, Noah and Rebekah. Peter recently took part in counseling victims and families of World Trade Center disaster victims.

Ned is a graphic artist working with a design studio, and on numerous freelance projects. He has greatly helped in the design and production of this book. He and his wife Tracy have two children, Jake and Grace.

Through the years and with our boys I managed to keep busy athletically by doing a lot of skiing with them and playing a lot of golf and tennis.

Most of my tennis was played with a group of men who got together every week during the summer and winter. These were George Little, David Thompson, Gil Rood, George Singer, and Bob Cochran. One bad eye closed out my tennis career a few years ago.

The Burlington Country Club is the scene of all my golfing. I played about once a weekend while I was working but since my retirement I manage to play about three times per week. My golfing buddies are Frank and John Cain, Ev Bailey, Proc Page, Phil Hoff, Frank Balch, John Carpenter, Gardner Soule. Sadly two others – Dick Mock and Jim Ritchie – have since passed away and we miss two great friends.

Being back in Burlington and in the shadow of the University of Vermont, I was fortunate to continue my involvement with UVM. I was a member of the board of trustees for six years, as was my business partner George Little. Quite often some of us alums get together for lunch.

Burlington, Vermont Friends in World War II

Richard Mock – U.S. Air Force

Dick Mock was always the guy who kept score and knew everybody else's when we played in our frequent golf foursomes. Being a flier he was always aware of the current weather and could forecast what was going to happen within the next half day. He always got the starting times and you could count on him for everything.

He enlisted in the Air Force and entered the service on March 16, 1942. After flight training and being commissioned, he flew with the 134th Fighter Interceptor Squadron, participating in combat missions in the European and North African Theaters. Dick flew 57 combat missions.

On one of the occasions after golf and a few beers, Dick related one of his experiences. On his 57th mission over Hungary his plane was hit and on fire. He had a bullet through the leg and flames all around. He finally ejected and the flaming plane crashed. He was

Howard Vreeland, Torrey Carpenter, John Royer, Bill Sisson, me and George Little, at the Burlington Country Club in 1999.

captured by the enemy and was a prisoner of war for 18 months. At that time and in that area there was constant and difficult interrogation. He remembered some beatings and occasional bread and water rations. He endured, however, and at the end of the war was released.

His medals and commendations included the Distinguished Flying Cross, Purple Heart, and the Air Medal with 14 Oak Leaf clusters. He had been on active duty from March 16, 1942, to January 6, 1946, and from February 1, 1951, to October 31, 1952. He was in the Vermont Air National Guard from November 1, 1952, to August 31, 1980, when he retired as a lieutenant colonel.

Several years ago while vacationing in Florida he contacted an infection and pneumonia. Serious complications followed and he passed away. We all attended his funeral in Burlington and the Vermont Air Guard honored him with a fly over of the cemetery during the 21-gun salute. There were no dry eyes among us and we'll always remember a great golfer, friend, and patriot. His widow Louise graciously shared some of his service records and recollections with us.

Francis Cain – U.S. Navy

Frank graduated from St. Michael's College in 1943, volunteered for the Navy, and went to Great Lakes Midshipmen School in Chicago. His first duty as an ensign was in the amphibious navy and he was assigned to the *LST 1* as a small boat officer. His duties were to handle one of the LCVPs during invasions.

While in the Mediterranean Theater when his ship was in the port of Palermo, Frank and I met at the officers' club one night. This was a great surprise to both of us, as neither of us knew the other was in the area. I was with the harbor clearance salvage unit in Palermo at that time. This happened to be at an officers' dance where not surprisingly, we met at the bar.

Later in the evening while I was dancing with a nice little Sicilian girl, some navy lieutenant cut in on me and danced with my partner.

Frank noticed this and after the dance we both edged up to the lieutenant to chat with him. Oddly enough this guy turned out to be a graduate of St. Michael's College named Lieutenant Lesage so our encounter ended up in a draw – a perfect example of friendly fire. It was great to see Frank so far from home; unfortunately his ship took off the next day as they were headed up to England to participate in the landings at Normandy.

The *LST 1* and its assault boats landed on Sword Beach in Normandy on D-Day, June 6, 1944. Following the invasion there were continuous back and forth trips from England to the French beaches with troops and materiel for the following five months, usually in the nasty weather typical of the Channel. The *LST 1* returned to the United States in February 1945 and Frank was assigned to the *LST 309* for a year's duty in the Pacific Theater. He was the last commanding officer of that ship, that was decommissioned in San Fransisco in June 1946.

After the war Frank returned to Burlington, married Jane Allen, and had ten children. He began his own insurance business and later merged with a larger firm. From 1965 to 1971 he was mayor of the city of Burlington. He participated in the urban renewal project

Everett Bailey, Frank Cain and myself in 2002.

that revised a major part of Burlington from Church Street to its beautiful harbor. Passing up a fourth term, he returned to the insurance business.

He did make a political exception in 1974 when he ran for Vermont's only seat in the United States House of Representatives. His opponent at that time was none other than Jim Jeffords, then the Republican candidate. Frank handily won the Democratic nomination and was pitted against the Republican incumbent. He did well but lost by about a 60-40 percent margin. Had Frank been elected, the political history of the country might have been significantly different than it was during the most recent defection of Jeffords from the party of Lincoln. If Frank had gone to Washington I would have missed the many years that we shared bowhunting and the countless rounds of golf we continue to enjoy.

John Cain – U.S. Air Corps

Frank's younger brother John was in the U.S. Army Air Corps as a gunner on the B-17 bomber. On one of his missions on March 18, 1945, his bomber was shot down near Berlin and he parachuted from the burning plane. Some of the German villagers who closed in on him as he lay in a gully were intent on killing him. After our continuous bombing and destruction of homes and the killing of thousands of German civilians the enraged populace were killing downed airmen. Fortunately a passing column of SS soldiers saved him. Unlike the villagers they had discipline and a code of conduct for dealing with captured enemies. Two of his friends from the same plane landed elsewhere and were murdered by civilians.

He was held in a prisoner of war camp in Germany until war's end. While in this prison camp he ran into another UVM graduate, Paul Corley, whose plane had been shot down earlier. John is another one of my golfing buddies and he, with Frank, Dick Mock, and I made up a foursome that golfed regularly.

The Carpenter Brothers – Don, John, and Torrey Carpenter grew up in Burlington. Through my years at the University of Vermont and after the war they all became friends of mine.

Don Carpenter – U.S. Navy

Don was the oldest and graduated from the University of Vermont in 1938. He entered the U.S. Naval Reserve in September 1942 and completed indoctrination training at the Naval Training School in

Newport, Rhode Island. While the members of this graduating class were often referred to as "90-day wonders," they actually finished their intensive training in two months.

His first assignment was as a Communications Watch Officer at Staff Headquarters of the Western Sea Frontier, in San Francisco. He then served as Communications Liaison Officer for the staffs of Convoy Commodores in the Asiatic/Pacific Theater. When World War II ended on the 14th of August 1945, he was serving aboard the flagship serving as a CLO., and Beachmaster for the CULA expedition in the Arctic waters off Point Barrow, Alaska.

He was separated from the service on February 26, 1946, remaining in the U.S. Naval Reserve. He was Executive Officer and then Commanding Officer of the Naval Reserve MSTS Unit, located at Treasure Island, California. On June 30, 1968, he retired with the rank of Lieutenant Commander., U.S.N.R. Don refers to his service career as "The Secret Blue Collar War."

His military awards include the Commendation Ribbon, World War II Victory Medal, Naval Reserve Medal, American Area Campaign Medal, the Asiatic Pacific Area Campaign Medal, and Reserve Officers Association Medal. He passed away on February, 2003, in Burlington, Vermont.

John Carpenter – U.S. Marine Corps

John graduated from Trinity College in Hartford, Connecticut, in the Class of 1941. In that summer he accepted a school teaching job in Arizona.

In May of 1942 he decided to forsake his schoolmaster post in Tucson and enlist with the fighting leathernecks – the marines. He went to basic training and boot camp at the San Diego training base and Camp Eliot in California. He began his overseas odyssey in October 1942, passing up Officers Candidate Training School and an opportunity for a commission in order to push off with his division.

Their first campaign was the Guadalcanal operation January 4,

1943, through February 19. The objective of this critical operation was the airfield, which the Japanese had started. After the marines had cleared the Japanese away the airfield was quickly completed. This airfield was significant for the operations in the southern Solomon Islands.

Their next operation was Tarawa, in the Gilbert Islands, on the 20th of November, 1943. He escaped death by scant inches, the heavy Japanese fire all around, as the marines hit the beaches and their landing craft became hung up on the coral reefs. "I reached around for my canteen only to find no water in it. A Japanese bullet had torn right through the bottom of it, but I never knew it. There were some holes in my pack, too. I had dug down in the coral but apparently that still left something of a target above the water." The Tarawa fight was over in less than a week. Saipan was next.

"The Japs were ready for us on Saipan," John said. "They pinned us down on the beaches for two hours with murderous artillery fire before our group could move inland. Their artillery, located in the hills, had apparently been trained on the beaches for some time expecting just such a landing, so accurate was their fire." A shell exploded so close that John was knocked out for a few minutes. When he came to, the other marines who had been near him at the time of the explosion, had disappeared. "To this day I don't know whatever became of them, whether they were blown to pieces or what happened. I never saw them again."

Assigned to regimental intelligence, he had to man observation posts during a campaign. "The long nights were the worst of all. It seemed as if they would never end as you prayed for the dawn of another day." In theory, one man was supposed to watch while the other sharing the foxhole slept. "Of course you didn't sleep as you crouched in a foxhole wondering what dangers might be creeping toward you. You hit the beaches with rifle in your left hand, spade in right, and heavy pack on your back. From then on, it was dig in, dig in, dig in. You dug a new foxhole every night."

It was during one of these nights that Corporal Carpenter and his foxhole mate captured a Japanese prisoner. He had blundered into their foxhole. It turned out that the Japanese soldier had a serious wound, became lost from his own unit, and wandered into their lines. The next day his wound was cleaned, and the infection reduced.

John miraculously came through it all unscathed, only to fall prey to an acute case of arthritis in the left knee, after the Marines had secured Saipan and Tinian and the fighting was all over for them. The "old man's" knee sent him to a Naval Hospital in Hawaii and finally to a succession of hospitals in the United States for treatment. Between several of the campaigns he had spent nine months, for R&R, training and maneuvers in New Zealand. He was discharged on November 2, 1945, at Great Lakes NTS, Illinois.

John's medals and commendations include the Presidential Unit citation for Tarawa and the Asiatic Pacific Area Campaign Medal with four Combat Stars. As a member of the 6th Marines, 2nd Marine Division he had served three years and six months as a great fighting leatherneck. After the war he returned to Burlington married his beloved wife Connie and raised a fine family, Chris, Tag, Scott, Kim and Debbie. John and I are good friends, socialize, bowl and golf together.

Torrey Carpenter – U.S. ARMY

Torrey was the youngest of the three Carpenter brothers and was in the class of 1944 at the University of Vermont. He entered the service in February of 1943 and had his basic training in the quartermaster corps at Camp Lee, Virginia. After that basic training and the usual battery of tests, he showed an aptitude for languages and was shortly on his way to the German program in the ASTP at Fordham University. Proficiency in German was not unpredictable as his father taught German and coached tennis at the University of Vermont. While Torrey was in New York we got together occasionally when I was in the diving program at U.S. Navy Training School for Salvage.

Just before the program was disbanded Torrey went back to the quartermaster corps at Camp Lee, Virginia, and was assigned to truck driving school. He went from academia to truck driving but had lucked out because the ones left in the disbanded ASTP program were sent to the infantry.

He then went overseas with a motor pool and was stationed in England, France, Belgium and Germany. One day while in France he ran into Ed Blakely, another of our friends from UVM, who had just been liberated after his plane went down in France. That same day Torrey had heard from his mother that Eddie Blakely was missing in action. Naturally she was tickled to death to find out that Eddie was still alive.

While in Furth, Germany, because of his language background he was selected to become the supervisor of a German civilian ice-cream plant that had been taken over by the U.S. Army – a classic example of an assignment completely different from your expectations. Torrey had an egg allergy and consequently taught the Germans how to make sherbet. Some time after managing the ice- cream plant and going from 170 to 210 pounds he was sent back to the States and discharged January 12, 1946. Never did he expect that the cards he were dealt would land him in an ice-cream factory in Germany.

He re-entered the University of Vermont in April of 1946 with the realization that UVM, Burlington, and Vermont were special. He married his college sweetheart Dorothy Frazer in 1947. They raised a great family – Sarah, Case, Rink, and Sam – and lived two blocks from the house on Kingsland Terrace where Torrey was born. We see the Carpenters often and our friendship continues.

Lee Matte – U.S. Army

Staff Sergeant Lee Matte was drafted into the army in the year 1941 as one of the first draftees from Winooski, Vermont. Lee was 29 years old at this time and was immediately sent to Fort Devens, Massachusetts. He received his uniform and was outfitted in record time of somewhere under two minutes. Shortly afterward he was transferred to Fort Bragg and to the 26th Field Artillery, Ninth Division headquarters. At that station Lee drove the command car for Colonel Dawson as a corporal. Soon after that he was made a staff sergeant and spent approximately 18 months at Fort Bragg. During that assignment he was offered a commission and a transfer from that unit. However, he decided to stay with that unit and subsequently participated in the landings in North Africa. His primary assignment was as a range survey for the gun battalions. He participated in the battle of El Gator. Shortly after that he found himself with a bad case of food poisoning in the field hospital. He was to participate then in the battles at the Kasserine Pass. He also said that in all of the original battles, the Germans used the Italian troops for frontline exposure. Lee lost his father when he was in Africa, leaving his mother a widow with 11 children.

At some point he was used as a liaison in a small town in Algeria with the mayor of that city. Lee was very fluent in French, so of course he was nicknamed "Frenchy." He was invaluable for his contact with the mayor. In my discussion with Lee he mentioned that when his unit hit the beach in their landings in North Africa they were instructed to proceed straight ahead, rendezvous in a cemetery, and seek shelter behind the monuments.

At one time Lee had allowed one of his privates to use his jeep. Somehow the enemy captured the jeep. The private who borrowed the jeep escaped and crawled back to the American lines. A set of dog tags of Lees were in the jeep when it was captured. Somehow or other the jeep was found and, thinking that he had been killed, someone shipped his dog tags back to the States. Needless to say his family was grief-stricken but soon found out that it was all a mistake and Lee had his original dog tags still around his neck. He later was shipped back to the States and had sufficient time in the service to be discharged. He then reported to Valley Forge for further assignment. At this point he was being considered for a commission but because he had left school at the age of 14 and had not had sufficient education, he did not qualify. At that time he was discharged and returned home.

He entered the printing business and ran the worthy competitor, the Merchants Press, until he retired. He passed away in 2002. All of us printers have fond memories of Lee.

Robert Lynch – U.S. MARINE CORPS

Bob "Caddy" Lynch was a neighbor of ours two doors from our first house. His wife, Mary, graduated with me from the University of Vermont. They have two daughters and a son who grew up with our children and were close friends of our family.

In June of 1942, Bob had enlisted in the U.S. Marine Corps and went to boot camp at Parris Island, South Carolina. He then reported on August 10th to Camp Lejeune, North Carolina, where he spent two months and was then sent to Camp Pendleton, California. On January 1, 1943, with the Ninth Regiment of 3rd Division they were sent to Aukland, New Zealand, for amphibious landing training. On March 1st, the 3rd Division, withstanding Japanese sub attacks, landed on Guadalcanal and did the mop up as the first and second divisions were relieved.

On November 1, 1943, they landed on Bougainville, the largest island in the Solomons group. On the beach, Staff Seargent Bob Lynch ran into my college roommate Lieutenant Misty Rice, shooting at Japs. On January 1st the 3rd Marines returned to Guadalcanal to prepare for their next operation.

On April 1st, the 3rd Marines hit Guam at Agana, and lost 600 marines the first day. While on Guam, a couple of our old friends, Larry Killick and Jim Fayette, got in touch with Caddy for a get-together at the officer's club. Caddy refused the offer as his ship back to the States was at the dock and he was raring to head back home. I later learned from Larry Killick that this party was a great Vermont Reunion. Eddie O'Connell, Red White, Jim Fayette, Windy Payne, and Larry celebrated old times at Eddie's Officer's club. They played "Moonlight in Vermont" all night on the Victrola, driving out Henry Fonda and others of Eddie's outfit.

Caddy's ship headed for San Francisco, and as they sailed under the Golden Gate Bridge, the war in Europe ended. They then headed for San Diego as Frisco was full of ships. On Mother's Day, May 15, Caddy called his mom to tell her his tour in the Pacific had ended.

Bob and Mary are now living in Saint Augustine, Florida, and we usually see them on their visits to Vermont.

Proctor Page – U.S. ARMY

"Proc" Page and I became close friends after I returned to Burlington in 1950. His sister Patty was a classmate of mine when I graduated from the University of Vermont in the class of 1943. Proc graduated from Dartmouth in May of 1942. He volunteered for the U.S. Army and entered the service on June 6, 1942. After basic training at Fort Dix, New Jersey, with the rank of corporal, he was assigned as an agent in the New York City Office of the Counter Intelligence Corps.

After a year he took a course in French with the view of service in the European Theater of Operations. However, he was assigned to the China, Burma, and India Theater of operations. He served mainly in India with several assignments in Burma.

In February 1945 he returned to the States and entered Infantry Officers Candidate School at Fort Benning, Georgia. After traveling halfway around the world the army decided that his eyes weren't good enough to lead a platoon in battle, disqualifying him. He was sent to the Military Intelligence Center at Camp Ritchie, Maryland, and was discharged in December following V-J day.

In 1947 he was in the Army Reserve unit at Fort Ethan Allen after having received a direct commission as a First Lieutenant. During the Korean War in 1951 he was called back to active duty in January. He was stationed at Camp Holabird, CIC Headquarters in Baltimore, Maryland. At that time his wife, Ruth, was pregnant with their second child and he was soon eligible for separation, with four dependents. He was discharged in October 1951.

I got to know Proc when he was in the printing business and publishing a newspaper in Essex Junction, Vermont. After we both retired we became golfing buddies and continue to be the best of friends.

Philip Henderson Hoff – UNITED STATES NAVY

With Governor Philip H. Hoff at Printer's Week signing

The first time I met Phil Hoff was on the golf course in Burlington, Vermont. It was 1952 and I had just joined the Burlington Country Club. Phil was also a new member and we were paired up for a round of golf. Neither of us played much golf as I was busy in the printing business and Phil was a young lawyer just getting started. His big interest was in politics and he subsequently got involved in the Vermont Democratic party. He was born in Turners Falls Massachusetts on June 24, 1924. In June 1943, while a student at Williams College, he volunteered for the Naval Air Corps.

Phil's account of this experience is as follows: "If you have trouble with coordination particularly in handling mechanical devices, and if you have problems with depth perception, what does a very patriotic 19 year-old do, you enter the Naval Air Corps." He attended flight schools in Glenview, Illinois and then at Chapel Hill.

"What happens thereafter is predictable. You ultimately have several accidents while landing airplanes and the Naval Air Corps finally decides to dispense with your services after one year." Phil then volunteered for the submarine service, went to the New London submarine training station and ultimately became a quartermaster on the USS *Sea Dog SS 401*, operating out of Subic Bay in the Philippines.

The *Sea Dog* initially operated out of Australia and was one of the first U.S. submarines to avoid Japanese mines and enter the Sea of Japan. At one point it ran aground but was able to free itself before the Japanese discovered it. This however happened before Phil came aboard in the summer of 1945.

After coming aboard the following incident occurred, as Phil related: "When the war ended, rumors abounded. One of them was that a Japanese submarine might surrender off the Philippines. Accordingly two men were dispatched from each submarine in Subic Bay (there were four subs), together with a very junior officer, to a Sub Chaser with orders to go out to sea and accept the surrender of any Japanese submarine that hove to. They strapped revolvers, 45s, around the waist of each of us even though none of us had any real experience with that weapon. All of us thought it was a lark and the eight crewmen immediately retired to the tiny dining galley to drink coffee and play cards. Then we hit the open ocean. A submarine in 300 feet+ is in a lot of water and quite stable. A sub chaser is quite small and anything but stable."

"We didn't stay long in the galley after we hit the open ocean and quickly returned to the deck and fresh air. While we were all queasy, none of us was sick. Not so for our junior officer. He stayed amidships and was violently ill throughout the entire day. I've often laughed at what might have happened had we in fact had a Japanese submarine hove to and surrender to us. First, not one of us knew a word of Japanese. Second, our officer in charge was so sick that he barely knew his name. Third, none of us knew anything about the operation of a Japanese sub. Can you imagine the reaction of the Japanese commander to this motley crew of American submariners?

Phil Hoff was discharged from the Navy in January of 1946. He returned to Williams College and graduated in 1948 and subsequently Cornell University Law School with a law degree in 1951. He married his lovely wife Joan, and headed for the Green Mountains of Vermont to raise four daughters.

His interest in politics continued and in 1960 he won a seat in the

state House of Representatives. He was the Democratic gubernatori-
al nominee in 1962 and broke a century of Republican rule becoming the first Democratic Governor of the state of Vermont. Phil
served as governor for six hyperactive years. He stepped down as
governor in 1968 and ran unsuccessfully for the United States Senate
in 1970, later becoming chairman of the state Democratic Party.
In the 1980's he returned to politics, serving in the state senate.

Through the years Phil and I have played a lot of golf together.
One year our foursome, and wives, went to Ireland to play golf and
see the Emerald Isle. One of our groups consists of Phil, Frank Cain,
the ex-Democratic Mayor of Burlington, and Everett Bailey and
myself, two somewhat Conservative Republicans. Some serious golf,
but no politics.

Kenneth Sprague Rothwell – U.S. ARMY

Ken and I first became friends when we were part of a group of
guys who played tennis weekly (often weakly at times). He was an
English professor at the University of Vermont and specialized in
Shakespeare courses. He is renowned for his writings and the study
of the works of Shakespeare and his many incarnations in the cine-
ma. He recently published a book titled *Shakespeare in the Movies.*

He entered the service on July 1, 1939, as a private in the 52nd
Coast Artillery, Fort Hancock, New Jersey. Then followed a one-year
special enlistment for competition to enter the United States
Military Academy from the enlisted ranks. He was discharged June
30, 1940 (without an appointment to the Academy). He received a
principal appointment to West Point, Class of 1945, in February
1941. He unfortunately failed the physical examination because of
high blood pressure and was not admitted to the academy.

He volunteered in July 1942 and was assigned as Private, L
Company, 349th Regiment, 88th Infantry Division, Camp Gruber,
Oklahoma. He was promoted to Sergeant, rifle squad leader in
August 1942. He qualified for Officers Training School and was sent
to the Infantry School, Fort Benning, Georgia in January 1943. Ken

was commissioned a Second Lieutenant of Infantry on April 10, 1943. He was permanently assigned as Rifle Platoon Leader to K Company, 159th Infantry, 7th Infantry Division, Fort Ord, California, in March 1943. In preparation for the Attu invasion, the division had been trained for North African warfare in the Arizona desert. It was then quickly retooled as an amphibious division under the tutelage of Marine Corps General "Howling Mad" Smith.

The battalion landed on Attu May 2, 1943 to relieve K Company, 17th Infantry, that had fought against the fanatical Japanese in ice, snow, and mountainous terrain. In July his regiment was left to garrison Attu, while the rest of the 7th Division went to Hawaii to prepare for the landings at Kwajalein, the Philippines, and Okinawa. For the next 20 months Ken's regiment patrolled the island of Kiska, where the 10th Mountain Division had been shipped for that operation only to find out that the Japanese had spirited all their men off Kiska. They also were sent to Amchitka Island where they aimlessly patrolled in search of the already vacated Japs.

On December 15, 1944, they received orders to return to the States with immediate reassignment to the European Theater. They were diverted to Camp Swift, Texas, and given short leaves to go home. The battalion was broken up and Ken was sent to Camp Shelby Mississippi to organize an Infantry Advanced Replacement Training Center.

In Ken's words –

After that there was a brief interlude at Camp Chaffee. Arkansas awaiting reassignment to a division to be shipped out for the invasion of Japan, which, as with most of my career, never happened. I could call my wartime record as 'one that never happened.

There was nothing left for me to do but take the G.I. Bill and get a Ph.D. to avoid ever having to work for a living.

Ken earned the Asiatic/Pacific ribbon with one campaign star. He was promoted to First Lieutenant and discharged in February 1946. Ken said he was the most senior second lieutenant in the army.

A great guy and one of my most unforgettable characters.

Willie Racine – U.S. Air Force

I met Willie after I got back to Burlington, Vermont, and was in the printing business. When we built our new printing plant we moved to Pine Street that was not far from Racine's auto repair garage. George and I always took our cars to Willie's place as we could count on him for excellent service. Later on he took on the Jeep franchise and moved to a new location. He is now retired and his sons continue to run a very successful business. His oldest son Doug was the Lieutenant Governor for the state of Vermont and most recently a candidate for governor.

Willie volunteered for the United States Air Force and entered the service in March of 1943. After his training he was sent to the European Theater and flew 35 missions as a tail gunner on the B-24 Liberator Bombers. He was awarded the Good Conduct Medal and Air Medal with five Oak Leaf Clusters. He was discharged in October 1945.

Gardner Soule – U.S. Marine Corps

I became acquainted with Gardner as he was a member of the Burlington Country Club and a friend of many of my fellow golfers. During the winter he and his wife Sally, a state senator, go to Sanibel Island, Florida. When we go south we play an occasional round of golf and do some socializing with the Soules. He originally came from Rochester, New York, and attended Williams College.

In 1943 he volunteered for the marines and went through boot camp and training at Parris Island and Quantico. In August of 1944 he joined the Sixth Marine Division as it was forming on Guadalcanal. Embarking on the *APA 219* in the headquarters battalion, he participated in the invasion of Okinawa on April 1, 1945, Easter Sunday, the last major battle of World War II. The American force was 287,000 strong of that over 60 percent were combat troops in four Army infantry and three Marine divisions. The U.S. forces soon encountered the massive Japanese fortification system inland. The blood bath had begun and continued until June 22nd when the battle was declared over. The division returned to Guam around July 5th to prepare for the ultimate invasion of Japan. On the sixth of August the first atomic bomb was dropped on Hiroshima by the B-29 *Enola Gay*. On August 14th the Emperor of Japan agreed to an unconditional surrender. The Sixth Marines performed some occupational duties in China. On January 15, 1946, Gard returned to the States and on March 16th was discharged. In 1951 he did some reserve training and in 1956 retired as a Captain in the United States Marine Corps.

Benjamin F. Schweyer – U.S. ARMY

I first met Ben Schweyer when I returned to Burlington in 1950. He was a lawyer in Burlington and also belonged to the Burlington Country Club.

In 1943 when he was a cadet at Norwich University he enlisted in the Army Reserve. He was called to active duty February 4, 1944. After 17 weeks of basic training he joined the 78th "Lightning", Infantry Division at Camp Pickett, Virginia.He was a Seargent in the 303rd Engineering Battalion. The 78th was shipped overseas in October 1944. They were in contact with the German Army for 125 continuous days. This included the Battle of the Bulge, the Remagen Bridgehead and the Ruhr Pocket, which all lay along the road to Berlin.

After six months of occupation duty the division was officially deactivated in May of 1946. Ben returned to the States and was discharged April 13, 1946. He wore the European Theater Ribbon with 3 Battle Stars and the Distinguished Unit Badge was awarded to all the members of his platoon.

I see Ben quite often on the golf course and we socialize occasionally with him and his lovely wife Margot.

Arthur J. Rock – U.S.ARMY

Art Rock is the only guy that I know who was born on the same day as I was, February 15, 1921. We are next-door neighbors as he lives in the same condominium complex as my wife and I. We went hunting together for many years and still play an occasional game of golf.

He was inducted into the army on October 14, 1942, and had his basic training at Camp Attabury, Indiana, and Breckenridge, Kentucky. As a member of the 83rd Infantry Division, 329th Infantry Regiment, he left the states on April 6, 1944, and sailed to Manchester, England, for additional training

The 329th Infantry left Southampton, landed in France on D+17 (June 23, 1944) and moved to the assembly area of Bricqueville where they relieved the 101st Airborne Division.Through the next month, encountering heavy resistance by German paratroops and SS troops, they assaulted fortified hedgerow positions and decimated the 17th SS Division. Following the withdrawing enemy, the regiment went into an assembly area in Fougères.

They then fought two major battles liberating St. Malo and swept down the Loire River where they bottled up 60,000 Nazis. Then on to Luxembourg, the Hurtgen Forest, the Ardennes,across the Rhine to the Elbe river, 65 miles from Berlin. At this point they met the Russians and were relieved two days before V-E Day.

Throughout this campaign, traveling 1,408 miles, Staff Sergeant Art Rock with Regimental Headquarters Company, earned the European, African, Middle Eastern Theater medal with 4 battle stars, and the Bronze Star. He returned to the United States and received his honorable discharge on October 10, 1945. We get together frequently with Art and his wife Pat.

Frank Balch – U.S. NAVY

I met Frank Balch in the early 50s when I returned to Burlington to go into business with George Little. Frank was with the local radio station WJOY doing sports announcing and other related radio work. Since then we became friends, played some golf together, Co-Coached a Little League baseball team, when our kids were young, and in general socialized.

He was only 15 when Pearl Harbor happened and still in high school. When he turned 17, he convinced his father that if he would let him quit high school and enlist in the navy he would promise to finish school after the war. He enlisted in the navy at age 17 and in September of 1943 went to boot camp in Newport, Rhode Island Radio School, and then amphibious training at Fort Pierce, Florida. He was assigned to the USS *Aurelia*, AKA newly commissioned, and sent directly to Pearl Harbor. Carrying troops and supplies to Eniwetok, Guam, and Saipan they ended up in the Philippines at Leyte Gulf and began preparing for the invasion of Okinawa. On April 1, 1945, on Easter Sunday morning, they were involved in the initial landings and subsequent suicide bombing attacks by kamikaze pilots. While there, President Roosevelt died and Frank copied the message in the radio shack ordering all ships not in the battle zone to lower their flags to half mast. After Okinawa, they returned to Pearl Harbor when the war ended August 14, 1945. Shortly thereafter they left for Japan with occupation troops to Sasebo, on Kyushu. They finished their tour in the "Magic Carpet Fleet," transporting army and navy personnel from various Pacific ports back to the states. On October 14, 1945, one year after his ship's commissioning, they had logged 50,130 miles cruising the Pacific.

After being discharged in April 1946, still shy of his 20th birthday, he rang the front doorbell in Lynn, Massachusetts, and when his dad came to the door he said, "I'm back to finish high school" – and he did.

Gilman Rood – U.S. AIR FORCE

Gil Rood was in the Class of 1941 at UVM and volunteered for the Marine Air Corps on July 19, 1941. After training at Quonset Naval station, in the same class as Joe Kennedy, he received his wings and on January 7, 1943, was sent to the Hebrides Islands during the Guadalcanal Operation. When the Marines secured the airstrip at Guadalcanal, he was among the first pilots flying the new Vought Sikorsky Corsair planes to land there. He was with flight squadron

VMF 124. The head of his squadron, Major Gise, with three other pilots, was lost during these operations. He then returned to the States for approximately a year to be spent in training other pilots.

After joining the new flight squadron VMF 133, Gil returned to the Marshall Islands preparing for the Okinawa operation, which began on April 1, 1945, Easter Sunday. On the second day the Japanese airfield was captured and friendly aircraft could begin operating from it. The planes in Gil's squadron were catapulted off a carrier headed for Okinawa. His group of 5 or 6 planes took off with instructions to land on the newly secured airstrip. Somehow they soon became aware that they had miscalculated their position, overshot the island, and were heading farther away from the target area. Being the lead plane, he reversed direction and soon they luckily spotted the lights of the Okinawa airfield. The group finally landed with practically empty gas tanks.

Gil wrote a candid synopsis of his naval career in a note to me as follows:

> *Luck! I went in as an immature jerk – Came out – Luck! Perhaps slightly less so. Memorable moments – the thud of a Zero's bullets into my armor plated seat. Luck! Sitting on a carrier deck watching a Kamikaze coming in low on the water. Like a sitting duck. Luck! A night attack on the Okinawa airfield by a transport filled with Jap suicide troops with no idea of what was going on. Luck! Being lost in bad weather over the South China Sea. Luck! The thrill of shooting down an enemy plane. Luck!*

Shortly after the Okinawa campaign the war ended. Gil came home to the States and was discharged in December 1945.

After the war when I came back to Burlington, Gil was in a tennis group with me and five other guys. We had weekly matches and had great times. Gil passed away in 2001 and is greatly missed by all of his friends.

William P. Dillon – U.S. Army Air Corps

I first met Bill Dillon when I moved to Burlington in 1950. We socialized and played golf together. When he married Joan Herberg, I was one of the ushers.

Bill enlisted in the army in 1942, and was discharged March 25, 1946. During World War II he was in the Army Air Corps in the Burma/India Theater. His primary duties were guiding the planes into the airport by use of ground to plane hookups. These were the planes that participated in the very dangerous flights over the Himalayas – the "hump" – during World War II. He was a radio operator and direction finder in the area communications systems. He spent approximately 12 months in the Burma/India Theater.

We were close friends with Bill and his family, and I was the godfather to a child. He passed away in 2002. We still see his wife Joan, getting together often.

Cy Williamson – U.S. Army
Hopkinsville, Kentucky

I met Cy Williamson on our first trip to South Seas Plantation Resort , on Captiva Island, Florida, in 1982. Since then we have been seeing Cy, and his wife Annie, on our visits there during February and March. Cy and I did a lot of fishing, golfing, boating, and great socializing on these visits. We never talked much about World War II but I knew that Cy had been wounded during his army career in 1944. This past year I told him about the World War II memoirs I was writing about many of my friends, and gave him some questions he said he'd answer. The last few years we were down there his health had been failing and a bad back had discouraged him from golfing, boating, and fishing. We did, however, manage our usual gin and tonic gab fests. We last saw Cy and Annie when they returned to his beloved Kentucky last year. We had a few phone conversations after that but in late June we received the sad news that Cy had passed away. Several weeks after that I spoke with Annie and she gave me most of this information about Cy's army career.

Cy graduated from the Citadel in 1943. He had been deeply interested in military life and his experience at the Citadel prepared him for his service in the Army. Right after graduation he enlisted in 84th Infantry Regiment of Kentucky, referred to as the "Rail Splitters." After training and maneuvers, the 84th landed in England on September 20, 1944. After less than a month preparation they landed in France and were rushed to the front in Belgium, near Aachen. During combat in this area it was necessary for someone to personally communicate with headquarters and second lieutenant Williamson accepted this assignment. Under constant shelling he carried out this assignment, but was wounded by shrapnel on a return trip on Thanksgiving Day, 1944. Badly wounded in the shoulder, he was sent back to England, and went through a series of operations over a long period. He was discharged as a first lieutenant some time after returning to the States.

A source of great pride to Cy is the fact that his grandson Matt enrolled at the Citadel. He recently graduated after having been selected for the famed Citadel Drill Squad.

Our visits to Florida will never be the same and we will always remember Cy and Annie and the wonderful times we had at South Seas.

The Docs

The roles played by the medical profession during World War II have in many cases been greatly overlooked. Because of the great need for doctors most of them volunteered for the services and finished their medical educations. The graduates immediately began their duties and assignments all over the world. I am including some of my close friends, relating their experiences in the service.

Gino Dente, Gordy Page, Platt Powell

Three of these doctors who have retired from active practices play golf regularly at our country club. Gino Dente, Gordy Page, and Platt Powell play in a threesome four times a week. Platt is 90, Gino is 85, and the youngster Gordy is only 84. Generally they play nine holes but occasionally on their high testosterone days they go eighteen. They don't keep score because Gordy told me that it spoiled his golf concentration. They all served in World War II and following are the stories of their service careers.

Gino Dente, M.D. – UNITED STATES ARMY

Gino graduated from the University of Vermont in 1941. He interned at the Freen Point Hospital in Brooklyn, New York. After Pearl Harbor Day he was inducted into the U.S. Army in May of '42 and was sent to the 13th Refresher Medical Group at Carlisle, Pennsylvania. They were then sent to Presidio, San Francisco and embarked on the USS *Etolin* with 90 other medical and dental officers to Honolulu, Hawaii.

The 24th Infantry Division then went to Queensland, Australia to train for the future engagement with the Japanese in New Guinea, Leyte, Luzon, and Mindanao. His duties during the first phase was as a member of the ambulance group of the medical battalion and then a member of D Company where they performed surgery on casualties. His duties were primarily in anesthesia and all minor surgery. The highly trained surgeons addressed all phases of major trauma. Primary protocol was to resuscitate. Nerve surgery was to locate and find areas of injury. Definitive repair trauma to brain was limited. Chest and lung injuries were to be life-saving, and definitive cases, sent immediately to hospitals.

In New Guinea he joined a MASH unit with a surgeon for four weeks. His unit was in bivouac in an old school house. One night as he was about to dig into his field pack for some cigarettes he thought to give it in a kick before opening. Out came a 3 foot snake that went for him. Dr.Tuttle, a surgeon with the MASH unit, grabbed his machete and slashed off the viper's head. The next morning on closer examination they found it was a cobra with hood and fangs.

In October of 1944 during the Battle of Leyte Gulf, one of the largest amphibious operations of the Pacific campaign, they saw their first Kamikaze planes. The light carrier, *Princeton CVL-23* was struck by a 500 pound bomb that penetrated into the torpedo storage, setting off a series of explosions, causing her to be abandoned and sunk. Their medical battalion kept busy when the casualties from the *Princeton* came in. Gino relates that one of their supply sergeants stole (borrowed) a generator, which allowed their surgeons to do more cases than they were originally equipped to perform.

In Mindanao the newly arrived doctor for one of the aid stations was killed and Gino was nominated to take his place. He proceeded with the jeep driver until they reached an area that was heavily mined. His driver said, "So long," and Gino was left to go it alone. He managed to make his way through that dangerous area before reaching his new outfit. This episode was later related to his own group and lead to his reception of the Bronze Star, which he says he received about 50 years after he returned home. His decorations included the Asiatic-Pacific Theater Ribbon with 2 stars, Phillipine Liberation Medal, and Meritorious Unit.

Captain Denti was discharged at Fort Devens, Massachusetts in 1946. He was on the Staff at the Veterans Hospital in White River Junction, Vermont and then at the Medical Center of Vermont in Burlington until his retirement.

H. Gordon Page, M.D. – UNITED STATES ARMY

Gordy Page was in the 1945 medical class at the University of Vermont having been in the ASTP program for two years. He interned at the Mary Fletcher and the Walter Reed Hospitals. He then served in Stuttgart, Germany, at the 23rd General Hospital until the war ended.

During the Korean War he was called back and reported to Fort Sam Huston in Texas for two days of basic training. Then on 24 hours notice half of the doctors were sent to Korea and the rest to Japan. Gordy was in the Japan group and they flew immediately to a large hospital in Osaka. At that time the Korean conflict was resulting in the evacuation of thousands of the wounded to Osaka. The Doctors were on a 12 hour on and off routine doing triage and emergency care. They were operating, and treating 3 to 4 thousand casualties a week. Gordy was on that duty for about a year and in 1951 he returned to Fort Devens where he was discharged as a major in 1951. He returned to Vermont and continued his career in surgery until retirement in 1990. He performed an appendectomy on my son Joe in 1970.

I see Gordy almost every day I play golf as he and his other doctor buddies play almost daily.

Platt Powell, M.D. – UNITED STATES ARMY MEDICAL CORPS

I first met Platt Powell when I returned to Burlington in 1950 when he was a practicing Urologist. He had been in the service until his discharge in 1946.

Platt attended the University of Vermont in the class of 1936, and the Medical School 1939. In my most recent contact with him he was kind enough to furnish me with the following summary of his World War II experiences:

I played saxophone in Joe Lechnyr's ROTC band for two years and had a reserve commission as a first lieutenant. After finishing academic and medical school plus internship in Philadelphia and a year with Dr. Buttles in pathology, I was called to active duty to Harbor Defenses of Boston at Fort Banks Hospital Winthrop. After several years I was transferred to the 136th Station Hospital, to England to take care of the 3rd Division, 8th Airforce.

The 136th was temporarily stationed outside New York City awaiting transport to England. We did a lot of physicals on units shipping overseas, then boarded the Queen Elizabeth with about 10,000 other troops. We sailed for Europe landing in Scotland four days later. Our unit boarded blacked out rail cars and reached our destination in East Anglia, Town of Long Milford, where we were near the 3rd Division of the 8th Airforce. The British had provided (taken over) a beautiful old brick farmhouse where our nurses lived, and an outbuilding for our officers. There were about 23 "Nisson Huts" for patients' care, operating rooms, Radiology, Diagnostic Neurology, General Surgery, Dental Surgery, and more. These wards would accommodate about 20 patients beds in each unit. We also had a Venereal Disease unit assigned to Medicine and Neurology. However, with the arrival of penicillin we were able to turn that service over to Medicine.

Patients came to us from a number of sources. American and B17 bombers flights would be seen gathering over the coast and when the designated numbers reached formation they would head out over the coast toward their assigned targets. After bombing, those able to return to their home base would often have injured personnel sent to our hospitals for treatment. Non-combat medical and surgical problems were also frequently seen. An occasional crash landing on return to England would have patients picked up by our ambulances.

Right after D-Day we began to receive casualties requiring further hospitalization, five to seven days after wounding, and treatment in a field hospital. My assignment, by request, was with Dr. Boris Petroff, a well-trained Urologist from a New York City hospital. He was a great guy and a pleasure to work with. On surgery we saw a lot of dirty wounds from the front, which required wet saline type soaks and antibiotics. Then when ready, resection of the wound and two closures.

If the wound was too extensive, or complicated and required more than 30 days of treatment the patient would usually be sent back to the states or to one of the General Hospitals in the west of England.

I should mention that we had the nurses, and the air force had the young officers and a supply of strong drinks. Some of our nurses, with a high-ranking nurse and an officer as chaperone plus an ambulance and driver were often asked to air force parties. We had the nurses and they had the scotch. Damaged planes would be "slow tuned" in Scotland for repair and restocking of their alcohol supply.

During one of these events my Superior Officer, while chaperoning, injured his heel quite severely jumping from the truck transport, repair would require more than a month. Hospital stay, and anything over 30 days was sent back to the United States for repair. Being next in command, I was now in charge of the entire section. If I had a problem needing consultation I could take the patient by ambulance to a General Hospital about 40 mi. away but never found it necessary.

As the war extended the Germans were firing unmanned "buzz bombs" from the Schelt-Estuary region of Holland that were targeted for London. I recall a night seeing one over our heads and a British Fighter on its tail pouring lead into it. It was brought down about a mile beyond our hospital.

Finally the war began to wane and it looked as though troops from the European fronts would be returning through the States to fight Japan. The Atomic Bomb over Japan changed all of this. Those of us with a lot of points would soon be home.

I returned again on the Queen Elizabeth and met my dear wife Marion at Fort Devens. Finally getting back to our apartment and kids in Milton, Vermont.

Platt Powell was one of those great physicians who saw first hand the terrible toll of young Americans who were wounded and died in World War II.

My wife and I enjoyed a trip with Platt and his wife Marion to New Zealand and Australia. We fished together on a lake in Rotorura, New Zealand where we caught some beautiful trout. We then visited the Great Barrier Reef, where Marion, Platt and I enjoyed some great snorkeling on those beautiful reefs. During the recent years we have been golfing friends at the Burlington Country Club. He recently had his ninetieth birthday and I phoned him my congratulations.

Wilfred Thabault

Wilfred Thabault, M.D.
– UNITED STATES ARMY AIR CORPS

On Pearl Harbor Day Willie Thabault was attending St. Michael's College. He was involved in the civilian aeronautical program at the Burlington airport. In 1942 he volunteered for the Air Corps but was turned down because of an eye problem that impaired his depth perception. He was given the option of joining the glider corps but decided to continue his premed program at St. Michael's, graduating in August 1943. He entered the UVM College of Medicine in January 1944 and joined the Navy B12 program for medical students. He graduated from med school in 1947 and went on to San Raphael hospital in New Haven, Connecticut, training in obstetrics and gynecology. At the end of his training he joined the U.S. Air Force, left the United States in July 1951 and was assigned to a hospital in Tokyo, Japan, during the Korean War. He was assigned to the team and treated the wounded. He served in Japan for three years and was discharged in 1954. He returned to Vermont and established himself in a practice of obstetrics and gynecology

Willie and I met some time after I came back to Burlington, Vermont, in 1950. We were both members of the Saint Michael's College Associates. Later on we played golf together and most recently are on the same bowling team at the Ethan Allen club. Our bowling team consists of four guys over 80 and one youngster of 76. Willie is legally blind, with some peripheral vision and is still able to bowl. We tell him what pins are left after the first ball and he remarkably is able to score very well.

He is married to Doris McNamara and they have nine children. Doris, now has Alzheimer's disease, and Willie and his family are lovingly taking care of her at home. Willie and I have lunch occasionally and continue bowling together.

Vermonters on the *Coolidge*

Dr. Henry M. Farmer **Rev. John Mahoney**
William A. Stebbins **Webster Thompson**

Lt. Webster Thompson, Major William Stebbins, Dr. Henry M. Farmer, and Father John Mahoney were all members of the 43rd Infantry Division in Burlington, Vermont. In April of 1988 the *National Geographic* magazine wrote an article concerning the 43rd Division and their ill-fated mission to the South Pacific. Following are some excerpts from this article:

> *The 43rd Division on about October 12, 1942, embarked on the* President Coolidge, *a luxury liner converted into a troop transport for service in World War II. With 5,440 men plus arms and equipment the ship crossed the Pacific in 14 days and was entering the harbor of Espiritu Santo in the New Hebrides Islands, the staging base for the hard-pressed Allied troops on Guadalcanal.*

> *First Lieutenant Web Thompson near the bow of the ship noticed a blinker light flashing on the shore but was unable to discern the message, which had been a warning that the* Coolidge *was headed straight for a mine field. "Suddenly there was an explosion followed by another," remembers Dr. Henry Farmer, "and the ship soon began listing."*

> *"The first word we got was that the ship wouldn't sink," remembers Major Bill Stebbins, "We were ordered to our duty stations."*

> *The captain of the* Coolidge *promptly ran the listing ship aground and 20 minutes later they got the word to abandon ship. They passed the word below decks. The men got lifejackets and started using the rope ladders. The port list complicated things. Starboard ladders didn't reach the water and some life rafts already lowered began drifting away. Stebbins recalls that "most of the men got off the ship in the last 20 minutes. I climbed into one of the last boats from a bow rope ladder."*

> *Dr. Farmer also crawled down a net and into a boat. Web Thompson and two non-coms slid down a rope off the fantail and into an empty raft. "When I got ashore I still had a crease in my pants," he recalls.*

Exactly one hour and 20 minutes after hitting the mines the Coolidge *settled on to the channel floor. Amazingly only five lives were lost, 5,435 were saved. Dr. Farmer treated the injured, which were mostly cuts and scratches acquired when they jumped from the ship. The most serious loss was the Atabrine, which was all the medicine available for malaria on Guadalcanal. In fact, the stranded men needed everything. "We had 900 men with nine rifles," said Web Thompson. "We borrowed a hundred mess kits from the Seabees stationed ashore. They had to totally equip the men who didn't get to Guadalcanal until March of 1943." The loss of the* Coolidge *delayed Allied operations by weeks.*

I knew most of the men referred to in the *National Geographic* story. Web Thompson is a friend who graduated from the University of Vermont in 1939 having taken advanced military and entering the service as a 2nd lieutenant. He served from September 1941 to March 1946.

I got to know Bill Stebbins around 1960 as he was the Manager of the Burlington Electric Company, a utility owned by the city of Burlington. As a member of that commission for 24 years, I was closely associated with Bill. He was a graduate of Norwich University in 1935 and commissioned a second lieutenant. He had a distinguished career with the Vermont National Guard and the 43rd Division during World War II. During his service with the Vermont National Guard he rose from first lieutenant in 1940 to Brigadier General in 1958 and was assigned in 1963 to the 86th Headquarters as Brigade Commander. In 1965 he was assigned as Assistant Attorney-General of the Army. In June of 1966 he was released to the Retired Reserve.

I knew Dr. Henry Farmer as he was a graduate of the University of Vermont and a member of the Kappa Sigma fraternity. He was also my physician on several occasions. Father John Mahoney and Doc Farmer were also brothers-in-law and I knew Father John as a local parish priest.

The whole saga of the loss of the *Coolidge* had an interesting twist as President Calvin Coolidge was a Vermont native son and the 72nd Infantry 43rd Division was part of the Vermont National Guard made up of many Vermonters.

"Jess" Jesse Vincent Fardella – US NAVY SALVAGE – *Coraopolis, Pennsylvania*

I am including Jess Fardella with my post war friends, as we have continued our navy friendship into our civilian life and kept in touch. Jess was living in Coraopolis, Pa., near Pittsburgh while I was in Buffalo, then Detroit and Burlington, Vermont.

Jess had graduated with a degree in mechanical engineering from Penn State College in State College, Pennsylvania. During his college years he was an active participant in the boxing program at Penn State under the tutelage of Leo Houck. Coach Houck led the

Nittany Lions to an NCAA title in 1932 and seven Intercollegiate Eastern Boxing Association titles in 26 years. In 1942, Jess was the Eastern Intercollegiate lightweight champion on the Penn State team. In those years, the match between Penn State and Navy at Annapolis was a major rivalry. The coming of the Penn state boxing team was an event that filled Navy's ancient battle shed to overflowing. Formal attire was a must and became commonplace at State College meets.

"Jess" Jesse Vincent Fardella

After graduating in 1943, he went to Notre Dame Midshipman School for two months. He then joined our class at the U.S. Naval School (Salvage) at pier 88 in New York where the French luxury liner Normandy, had burned and capsized on its side in the Hudson River. We shared an apartment together during diving school and went through the same rigorous diving training.

Jess Fardella and me

On March 10th, 1944, Jess, three others and I, received orders to report to the Eighth Fleet in the Mediterranean area. Via Casablanca, Algiers and Dellys, a small town near Algiers, we reported to Palermo, Sicily for harbor clearance work and salvage in that area. As we were both in the same diving crew in Palermo, our duties continued to be the same until June 30th, 1944 when I was assigned to the LCI 40 for the southern France invasion.

After I left the Palermo group they continued operations in Palermo, until after the invasion of Southern France when they were ordered to Toulon for harbor clearance in that devastated area. The entire unit packed all the salvage equipment on the USS *Tackle* and headed for Port De Bouc, in southern France near Toulon.

As they entered Port de Bouc the *Tackle* hit a mine. The ship was slightly damaged with the loss of one man. Jess and the men in this unit operated in Toulon harbor until early December when they were ordered back to North Africa. By that time I had been with them for several months and we all went back to North Africa together.

After North Africa and some pre-commission training in Newport, Rhode Island Lieutenant (jg) Fardella reported to Jeffersonville, Indiana for assignment to the *Laysan* (ARST-1) as Salvage Officer.

After their shake down off the Texas coast, the *Laysan* departed Galveston, Texas on July 17 for the Pacific. She transited the Panama Canal 25 July; touched Enwitok August 25, and arrived in Manila Bay, Luzon, September 6. The next seven months she operated out of Manila Bay.

During salvage operations in Manila Bay one of Jess's assignments was to work on a sunken ship in the harbor. For his work in the raising of this ship he was awarded the following citation;

> *The President of the United States takes pleasure in presenting the Navy and Marine Corps medal to:*
>
> *Lieutenant Jesse Vincent Fardella, United States Naval Reserve*
> *For services as set forth in the following citation:*
> *"For heroic conduct as the Assistant Salvage Officer during salvaging operations on Wreck No. 7 in Manila Harbor from November 19th, 1945, to January, 9,1946. Voluntarily diving into the water before enlisted men were permitted, Lieutenant (then Lieutenant, Junior Grade) Fardella went beneath the warped, torn wreckage of sharp steel on which his life lines might easily have caught and torn, and entered dark holds where there were gasoline and hydrogen sulfide vapors, which dangerous to the body, had exploded cargoes of gasoline and oil drums before, and now exploded frequently with his burning arc oxygen. His initiative, devotion to duty and outstanding courage were contributing factors in the successful salvage operations in Manila Harbor and reflected the highest credit on Lieutenant Fardella and the United States Naval Service.*
>
> *For the President,*
> *James Forrestal, Secretary of the Navy*

At the end of March 1945, Lieutenant Fardella received orders for discharge. He left Subic Bay Naval Base, returned to the United States and terminated his Navy career in Philadelphia, Pennsylvania.

After the war Jess and I kept in close touch. He visited me in North Tonawanda and I made several trips to Coraopolis. When he became engaged to Rita he asked me to be his best man. The Fardellas had one boy and three lovely daughters. Their son, Jess Jr., attended Yale University for his undergraduate studies and graduated from Harvard Law School in 1978 after which he worked as a clerk for a state Court of Appeals in Massachusetts. He was an associate at Ropes and Gray, a Boston law firm, for the next three years and then was persuaded by a friend to become a prosecutor for the U.S. attorney's office in Manhattan. In the summer of 1987, Jesse Fardella, then assistant United States Attorney, learned that he might be asked to join the investigation of Michael R. Milken and Drexel Burnham Lambert, Inc. With his co-prosecutor John Carroll they toiled to prove Milken broke the law through his junk bond business of Drexel Burnham and Lambert. Fardella at 38, and his partner Carroll 34, will forever be known for having nailed the biggest figure in corporate finance since J.P. Morgan.

Jesse V. Fardella was a significant part of my Navy experience and we continue our close relationship. He's one of the great persons in my life and it is a privilege to call him my friend and share these WWII memoirs.

COLLIER'S   "When we do a salvage job, we do a salvage job"   PAUL CARRUTH

Powell J. Whalen – USMC

Burlington, Vermont

When we played Lehigh University during the Southern Trip, Russ West, our shortstop, and I looked up a friend, Powell Whalen from Burlington, Vermont who was studying at Lehigh. Russ was in the same fraternity as Powell who was very gracious to us and we had dinner at his fraternity house. This was the last time I saw Powell until 1951 after I returned to Burlington. I had heard that he had joined the Marines right after college and had been badly wounded during World War II.

After returning to Burlington, one day while walking around Church Street I ran into Powell. He had changed. He was limping, walked unsteadily, and was slightly bent over. I shook hands with him and told him my name. He kind of stammered and finally did remember me and that last meeting at Lehigh University. He asked me about my brother Jim whom he also knew. It was obvious that Powell had been very seriously damaged by his injuries in the Marine Corps. He was a completely different person from the guy I knew during our college days – an example of a veteran who did return after the war but whose physical and mental capacity had been tragically diminished. He was currently working for some of the people in City Hall and capable of running errands, but had lost much of his short-term memory capacity. I met him several times after that and he would always remember to ask me about my brother Jim. He has since passed away, but I will always remember Powell and what World War II had tragically done to him and his loving family. He is a true hero embodying all the principles of the Marine Corps.

Following is a summary of the actions and subsequent occurrences during the period in which Powell was injured in action. This material was shared with me by his brother Kemener Whalen of Burlington, Vermont.

Powell was a Leader of an Engineer Platoon of Company F, Second Battalion, 25th Marines, Fourth Marine Division, in action against enemy Japanese forces on Saipan, Marianas Islands, June 17, 1944. These excerpts are from reports given by Corporals Boo, Davis and Private Irwin.

The time was 1100, day two. We received our orders to attack and they were executed. Our advance was halted due to fixed enemy fortifications, the engineers were called on, and Corporals Boo, Davis, Private Irwin and Mr. Whalen led the assault. Lieutenant Whalen leading, started over a knoll and was hit by machine-gun fire. Davis and Irwin assaulted the pillbox while Boo and part of F Company responded with supporting fire. After the assault Davis, Boo, and Irwin went to aid Whalen. Upon picking him up Whalen and Boo were wounded, Mr. Whalen for his second time in the head. He was taken to a safe area and corpsmen administered first aid to him.

This is a dispatch from October 20th, 1944, relative to the condition of First Lieutenant Joseph Powell Whalen, U.S.M.C

Lieutenant Whalen was admitted to the sick list 17th of June, 1944, immediately subsequent to having been struck in the head by fragments of enemy artillery fire on the island of Saipan, suffering from a compound fracture of the skull involving the left parietal bone with numerous fragments having been driven into the brain substance. He was evacuated to a hospital and on June 19, 1944, the wound was debrided and dressed. On June 25, 1944, he was admitted to the Naval Hospital in a serious condition. The skull wound appeared to be infected and he was again operated on with incision and draining of abscess in the skull wound. Penicillin was given to combat the infectious process, and he remained in a comatose state until mid-August during which time he was fed via a nasal catheter. He gradually showed some clinical improvement with mental clearing and orientation and on September 2, 1944, he was surveyed to the U.S. mainland for further disposition,

He was brought to the U.S. hospital on the 26th of September 19th, 1944, at which time examination showed a somewhat emaciated individual, quite well oriented but with definite defect of temporal and special orientation for past events. There was a partial apraxia present. A depressed defect of the skull, measuring one-and-a-half inches in

diameter, was present in the left parietal region. He had right hemi-
paresis and nystagmus to the left.

The progress to date has been satisfactory. There's been considerable
improvement in mental alertness, although he still demonstrates
marked memory difficulty. Some apraxia and childish emotional reac-
tions as well as hemiparesis are present.

He has had a few convulsive attacks, both general and Jacksonian
in type, but these have been controlled by medication. There has been
improvement in his mood, memory and the use of arm and leg. This
man is suffering from a destructive lesion involving the left pre-central
area. The prognosis of a mental functional recovery is guarded.

A Citation From James Forrestal Secretary of Navy:

The President of the United States takes pride in presenting the
Silver Star Medal to First Lieutenant Powell J. Whalen in United
States Marine Corps Reserve for service as set forth in the following:

"For conspicuous gallantry and intrepidity as Leader of an
Engineer Platoon of Company F, Second Battalion, 25th Marines,
Fourth Marine Division, in action against enemy Japanese forces on
Saipan, Marianas Islands, 17 June 1944.

While attempting to knock out enemy positions with demolition
charges and grenades, First Lt. Whalen unhesitantly lead three of his
men against a powerfully entrenched hostile strong point which was
holding up the company's advance, continuously exposing himself to
terrific Japanese fire in order to accomplish his mission. Wounded dur-
ing this heroic action, Lieutenant Whalen by his intrepid courage and
zealous efforts, contributed materially to the success of his company's
operations on this island, and his unfaltering devotion to duty
throughout was in keeping with the highest traditions of the United
States Naval Service."

For The President,

James Forrestall, Secretary of the Navy

Taps

I have related over a hundred of the countless World War II stories of many of the persons whom I have been privileged to call friends. We all heard the call to duty in many regions of the world, where fate destined that we serve our country in the pursuit of the freedom we all hold so dearly.

"The cards were dealt and we played our hands."

We served in the army, navy, army and navy air forces, marines, coast guard and all the individual branches of these services.

The total number of Americans who served in World War II was 16,112,556. Of these 405,399 died and 670,846 were wounded. Many are buried in cemeteries all over the world. The hundreds of thousands of white crosses in these cemeteries bear mute testimony to the young lives so early sacrificed in the defense of their country. Many of the sailors who died at sea were interred in the traditional navy custom, and relegated to the deep waters of the oceans.

Today, whenever a person is buried with military honors anywhere in the world, the ceremony is concluded by seven soldiers firing three volleys of musketry over the grave, and sounding with the trumpet or bugle, "Put out the lights. Go to sleep." There is something singularly beautiful and appropriate in the music of this wonderful call. Its strains are melancholy, yet full of rest and peace. Its echoes linger in the heart long after its tones have ceased to vibrate in the air.

"Taps" as composed by Major General Daniel Butterfield, Army of the Potomac, CivilWar:

Fading light dims the sight,
And a star gems the sky, gleaming bright
From afar drawing nigh, falls the night.
Day is done, gone the sun,
From the lake, from the hills, from the sky.
All is well, safely rest, God is nigh.
Then good night, peaceful night,
Till the light of the dawn shineth bright.

Acknowledgements and Thanks.

I have placed these memoirs into various stages of my life and the many friends made during those years. I then described their participation in World War II from information gathered through them and others including the widows and families of departed friends. —JEC

I wish to express my grateful thanks and appreciation to the following for their cooperation and research in furnishing the World War II biographical information on the Army and Navy baseball teams of 1942.

Kathleen. M. Lloyd – *Head, Operational, Archives Branch* and;
Beverly Lyall – *Archives Technician, Naval Historical Center, Department of the United States Navy, Washington Navy Yard, District of Columbia*

Sandra Tomczak – *Archivist for Research* and;
Cullum Files – *Association of Graduates, United States Military Academy, West Point, New York*

I am also grateful for permission to use excerpts from several published works:

Frank Braynard, *The Picture History Of The Normandie*

In a phone conversation on June 27, 2002, granted me permission to use any pictures or excerpts from that book in these memoirs. He specifically mentioned the great cooperation of Admiral Adolphus Andrews, Chief of the Third Naval District during the writing of his book.

In my writing of the segment on the USS *Squalus* I have used facts and excerpts from the book, *The Terrible Hours*, the story of the greatest rescue in submarine history, by Peter Maas.

I used other facts and information from: *The Century,* by Peter Jennings and Todd Brewster, and *The Pacific War Encyclopedia,* by James Dunnigan and Albert Nofi.

In the biographical history of my friend Lieutenant Jim Conant, I referred to the book *Take Her Deep* by Admiral I. J. Galantin, USN who was captain of the submarine *Halibut SS232* on which Jim served from 1943 until 1945.

In the biographical history of my friend Jud Decker I referred to the book *See Naples and Die* , by Robert B. Ellis. I noted some of the experiences of Jud in the 10th Mountain Division and their record in World War II .

The story of the Niland Brothers mentions some of the information found on the Internet relative to the movie *Saving Private Ryan.* Another source of information on the Nilands came from the book *Band Of Brothers,* by Stephen Ambrose. Fritz Niland's cousin, 85 year old Joe Niland, gave me permission to include the Niland story in these memoirs

The Willie and Joe cartoons are from the publication *Stars and Stripes,* and the book *Up Front* which is a collection of World War II cartoons by Bill Mauldin.

My special thanks to:

Grant Harris, a special friend, who served with me aboard the *Preserver* during my tour in the Asiatic Pacific theater. Grant provided the negatives of all the pictures that he took at that time.

John Criscuolo, of Brooklyn, New York, our Chief Yeoman who sent me the complete ship's log of the period during which I served on the *Preserver.*

My son Ned, who helped collect, edit and lay out this book from all the haphazardly narrated text that I dictated to my iMac™ computer using ViaVoice.™

My son Bruce, who helped with the images, many of which were digitized from the original negatives.

R. Scott Perry for editing assistance.

Many of my friends' widows and children who dug into their family archives and furnished much of the information concerning their departed loved ones. This wasn't easy for them, and I deeply appreciate their efforts. The contact with so many wonderful people renewed many of my precious memories of old friends.

Last, but not least, to my dear wife Mae, who tolerated the many hours I spent researching and compiling these memoirs.

Index to Names